This Must Be My Brother

This Must Be My Brother

LeAnn Thieman & Carol Dey

To Laurie,
Peace —
LeAnn Thieman

VICTOR BOOKS

A DIVISION OF SCRIPTURE PRESS PUBLICATIONS INC.
USA CANADA ENGLAND

Copyediting: Sharon Linnea, Barbara Williams
Cover Design: Scott Rattray
Cover Photos: Bettmann Archives, Peter Arnett, LeAnn Thieman,
Cedar Rapids Gazette

Thieman, LeAnn.
  This must be my brother / by LeAnn Thieman & Carol Dey.
    p. cm.
  ISBN 1-56476-383-8
  1. Vietnamese Conflict, 1961-1975 — Women. I. Dey, Carol.
II. Title.
  PS3570.H443T45 1995
  813'.54 — dc20   94-33193
                                                            CIP

1 2 3 4 5 6 7 8 9 10 Printing/Year 99 98 97 96 95

*Dedicated to Mitch
Thanks for choosing me*

Acknowledgments

With special thanks to Cheryl Markson for your phenomenal memory and assistance in providing facts and follow-up information.

Thanks to Ellen, Margaret, Lynn, Sally, Helen, and June for your wisdom and confidence.

Thank-you to W. Darryl Mehring for providing the initial encouragement to start this project.

And thanks to David Horton who never stopped believing in it.

Not flesh of my flesh
Nor bone of my bone
But still miraculously my own.

Don't forget for a single minute
You did not grow under my heart
   —but IN it.

                anonymous

Chapter One

A large ceiling fan hummed overhead as we sat in the Manila airport lounge shaking our heads.

"I can't believe we're stuck here for six hours," I complained to Carol. Could anything else go wrong to test our commitment to this trip?

"The truth is, the flight crew is unwilling to stay on the ground in Saigon any longer than absolutely necessary," a fellow passenger said as he joined us. "They're scared of the increased bombing around Saigon these past few days. That's the real reason for this layover."

Yet another piece of information to cast doubt in my mind.

"Why are you two ladies going to Saigon at a time like this, anyway?" asked another traveler as he sipped a cold drink. "The country's going to fall any day now."

His question was one we had asked ourselves a hundred times in the past weeks as we got ready for the journey.

"We're officers in the Iowa Chapter of an organization called Friends of Children of Vietnam," I answered. "FCVN raises money and collects supplies to send to Vietnamese orphans and processes adoptions. Whenever they have six or so babies ready for placement in the United States, they send chapter representatives to escort them home." I smiled

11

wanly. "At the moment, that's us."

But stuck here in the Manila airport, it was impossible not to dwell on how much things had changed since I had agreed to go. I'd met Cheryl Markson and Carol Westlake, the national officers, at the FCVN convention only two months ago. I was surprised—well, actually, "shocked" might be closer to the truth—when they called me a few weeks later to ask if I'd be an escort in April. Because of the time constraints, I had only twenty-four hours in which to give them my decision.

I knew the trip would have special meaning to me. My husband Mark and I had completed all our paperwork for an adoption through FCVN and had sent it to Denver just weeks before. The prospect made us both excited and nervous. Excited at the idea of bringing home a brother for our daughters Angela and Christie—but nervous that Vietnam would fall before the year-long adoption process was complete and our son brought to the States. I knew that even though I wouldn't be bringing our son home, I would be bringing children for other families. That in itself seemed justification for the trip. I agreed to go.

I looked at my friend Carol sitting next to me. As she told the men more about the purpose of our trip, I wondered if we could possibly look like anything other than what we were: two Iowa homemakers who'd rarely been out of the Midwest—let alone out of the country. But I smiled confidently and nodded agreement with a sense of conviction and support.

But it wasn't always so.

Carol and I had each struggled with our own personal demons between the time we made the commitment to go and the moment we actually boarded the flight in Iowa City.

When we had first agreed to go, the situation in Vietnam had seemed stable. Cheryl Markson, the national director of FCVN, had assured me that there had been no acceleration in the war for months and that we would be safe in Saigon. But as the paperwork to obtain visas was completed and our flight plans finalized, the final North Vietnamese offensive began. As we busied ourselves with the day-to-day details of caring for our children, arranging flights, getting immunizations, and obtaining passports and visas, our television screens showed maps of Vietnam and battles raging near Saigon.

Carol and I watched the news together, each in our own living rooms, connected by telephone lines and apprehension. "Abandoning a twenty-year policy of fighting for every inch of Vietnamese territory, President Nguyen Van Thieu has surrendered fully one fourth of his country—seven provinces—to the attacking communists."

"Did you hear that, Carol?"

"Turn it to channel seven and listen to this."

"General James Gavin said, 'The penetration of Saigon by the North is so great that what I get is a gloomy picture of Saigon's ability to save itself.' "

I cringed with fear and uncertainty.

To make matters worse, whenever the war was mentioned, my husband Mark looked at me meaningfully as if to make a point. He never asked me not to go, though I imagined the words were screaming inside him. Sometimes I wished he would have spoken them. It would have simplified things. I would then have had an excuse to back out as my misgivings grew.

We had always joked that he was the realist and I the idealist and that's why we were such a great balance for each other. Clearly, those virtues were dictating our feelings and actions in this dilemma.

Many husbands accompanied their wives on these escort missions, but I knew that would be out of the question for Mark. I had always prided myself in maintaining a balance between being a wife, mother, part-time nurse, and FCVN volunteer, but I sensed his resentment of the time this additional cause took me away from home.

13

I had been surprised one day in February when over a lunch of hot dogs and spilled milk with our children, Carol talked about going with me. Her husband, Al, often teased her about being less than adventuresome in their eleven years of marriage.

"Going to Saigon sounds like an exciting thing to do," she said, wiping catsup from the face of her two-year-old, Chad. "What a tremendous opportunity to see the orphanages in person and to bring the babies home to their new moms and dads." Because she and I were such close friends, Carol knew we would travel well together. "I've already discussed it with Al," she said, adding to my amazement. "He thinks it's a great idea and says he can manage the home front." His position as minister would give him the needed flexibility to oversee the kids. Not only that, he seemed confident she would be safe.

We sent our four children — my two daughters and her two sons — to the playroom and cleared the table. I waved the sponge in my hand. "It makes sense for me to go. My being able to tell our son that I was there and saw his homeland should be meaningful to him someday. I just can't believe you would really go with me."

We talked on between interruptions of tying shoes, wiping noses, and fixing toys. By the end of the afternoon we agreed we would go together.

At the time, it seemed rather exciting.

But as the departure date approached, Carol's and my confidence waned in direct proportion to our growing fears. Carol called the State Department nearly every day to ask for new developments. Each time they assured her it was okay to go, that we would be in no danger. Despite those assurances and the enthusiasm and support of her husband and friends, her fear began to build. She was more apprehensive than I, perhaps because she saw the reality of what we were doing and understood the physical jeopardy in which we'd be placing ourselves. I, on the other hand, was afraid, not of death or injury, only of the unknown — of leaving my familiar situation for a world I could not fathom.

The weeks flew by, taking with them any romantic illusions I might have harbored. Suddenly our day of departure was upon us, and there was no alternative but to face the fact we were about to board a plane to a foreign land — a land ravaged by war.

On Easter Sunday, the day before we were to leave, I went to church with my family, as usual. But as the service ended, I found myself in turmoil, more uncertain than ever about what to do. Mark must have read my unspoken need. He signaled that he would take the girls downstairs for donuts.

Soon the voices of the other worshipers receded and I sat alone in the empty sanctuary, embraced by the thick, sweet smell of Easter lilies.

I had always considered myself a religious person, but in a private sort of way. My daily prayers weren't formal but more like running conversations with God about family, friends, problems, or events of the day. If I hadn't trusted that He would take care of me, I never could have agreed to go to Saigon.

Now I knelt, trembling, fighting back tears. The courage that had kept me strong had fled. I rested my head on the pew in front of me. All the doubts and worries I had suppressed the previous weeks descended en masse, like a drenching rain. I could feel myself crumbling. I pursed my lips together hard to keep myself from crying out loud, but I could not stop the tears that trickled down my folded hands.

"What am I doing? I'm leaving everything I know and love, and for what?" My knees were too weak to support me so I sat back on the edge of the pew with my face in my lap. The sobs came.

"Please God, give me a sign that I don't have to go." I gasped to catch my breath, aware that the sound echoed in the empty church. There. I'd said it. Remembering the Scripture reading earlier I whispered, "Let this cup pass me by. Why does it seem You're asking me to do this? Please show me it's okay not to go."

Slowly, unexpectedly, a warm feeling enveloped me and my tears began to subside.

My breathing slowed to a deeper, calmer pace.

My shoulders and chest relaxed as an unexplainable feeling of well-being and courage filled me.

I knew then I was going to be okay.

Everything was going as planned.

I was meant to go to Vietnam.

He would take care of me.

"Thank You," was all I could manage to speak. I sat for a while soaking up the marvelous feelings of renewal, then left the church, my spirit soaring.

Carol called me that afternoon to say her fears had been eased somewhat that morning. She had attended her own church across town. After the service, friends and fellow parishioners had approached her—each offering words of encouragement. Afterward, another friend stopped by her home to find her nervously sorting her clothes, as well as her thoughts, for the trip.

"How are you doing?" her friend asked.

"I'm scared to death!" Carol had admitted. "It's so much more dangerous now than when we first said we'd go. I call the State Department every single day. They keep saying we should go. I want them to tell me to stay home!"

"Do you feel like things have fallen into place for this trip?"

She admitted they had. In fact, it seemed she was meant to go.

"Go then," he advised, "or you'll never know the impact you could have made."

"That's easy for you to say," she grinned. "You've traveled all over the world!"

Chapter One

"That's how I know you'll be fine. This is an opportunity of a lifetime."

"Of course you're right. I know I'll be forever disappointed in myself if I don't follow through with this."

By the time she called me, Carol admitted her anxiety was relieved . . . at least temporarily.

* * *

Even though our decisions were made, the good-byes the day we left Iowa City were difficult.

As I placed a few last items in my suitcase, I could hear the radio in the bathroom. Mark listened to the news as he shaved every morning.

"The Binh Long Province just fifty miles north of Saigon was relinquished to the Vietcong . . . there are reports of bombing within three miles of the Saigon city limits."

I closed my suitcase. Mark had come into the bedroom. He and I stared into each others' eyes, unable to look away yet unable to speak. He turned and left the room.

It seemed so strange not to be able to talk about all of this. We always prided ourselves in our great ability to communicate. On the rare occasions that we had disagreements, we stayed up hours into the night talking until our feelings were understood. Mark was not only my husband, but a confidant, a best friend. There was nothing I couldn't discuss with him.

Until now.

I hadn't told him of the incident in church the day before either. I had told no one. How could I explain it? And who could believe it anyway?

Before going to the airport, Mark and I took Angela and Christie to stay with my sister, Diane. Mark's work as a psychologist at the university meant long hours, and we were delighted that the girls could spend time with their aunt and uncle rather than in day care.

Angela was nearly four and seemed to understand when I

17

told her that I was going away for a week or two to help some needy children in the country where her future brother lived. I reminded her that I couldn't bring him home with me, that it would be a long time before he would come to us. I managed a grin as her long, blonde pigtails draped over us and we hugged good-bye. I could tell she too was forcing a smile.

"Bye, Mommy. I love you. I hope you have fun there." Her big blue eyes brimmed with love. No wonder we named her for an angel.

Christie was almost two and waited eagerly to hug me and hurry off to play. Her chubby cheeks pressed against mine, seemingly unaware of the emotion held in check. "I love you a bushel and a peck!" she giggled.

"And a hug around the neck," I answered.

I literally ached with grief as I left them. Yet I knew I was doing the right thing.

Mark and I rode, hardly speaking during the thirty-minute drive to the airport. What was there to say? I knew that if Mark spoke as openly as he usually did, he could only ask me not to go. He would never do that.

Carol and Al were waiting at the airport, standing in what seemed to be uncomfortable silence. Five-year-old Chris and two-year-old Chad, surrounded by the airport hustle and bustle, were excited. Chad clung to his mommy, though, with a bewildered look in his eyes. Carol told him she would be back soon. She probably needed the reassurance as much as he did. When the flight was announced she hugged and kissed each of them good-bye with a cheerfulness I knew was false.

"Thanks for being so supportive. I love you," she said to Al as she gave him a second hug. "I still can't believe I'm doing this."

I lingered in Mark's arms, reluctant to let go of the love and security I felt there.

"I'll assume you're okay unless I hear from the Red

Chapter One

Cross," he said reminding me that I wouldn't hear his voice again until I was on the way home. Since we realized that phone communication from Vietnam was unpredictable and difficult, we agreed that I wouldn't plan to call him.

"I'll be fine," I assured him. And I was sure of it. Since my experience the day before, I was filled with a newfound confidence. Still, as we walked across the open concourse to board the plane, I couldn't bring myself to look back and see the pain I knew must be reflected on Mark's face.

Once on board, I sat next to Carol, then forced myself to look out the window and blow him a kiss. He returned it, trying to smile. I leaned back against the seat and allowed the tears to fall.

Chapter Two

The two-hour flight from Iowa City to Denver passed in near silence. Neither Carol nor I had ever left our children for more than one night before.

The force of the emptiness I felt took me by surprise. It reminded me of the way I felt when my dad died. I reclined the airline seat, rested my head back, and tried to recount the chain of events that had snowballed into this commitment.

For as long as I could remember, I had wanted to adopt a child. As a matter of fact, I mentioned that desire to Mark soon after we were engaged. I was deeply affected by posters of starving children during the church's Thanksgiving clothing drives and school's UNICEF appeals. That desire to help is what had drawn me to join the FCVN chapter in Iowa City. Within a year Lauri, the chapter president, moved away, and my own basement became state headquarters. The handful of dedicated members raised money by selling baked goods, helium balloons, and greeting cards. We arranged baby showers to benefit the orphans and solicited sponsors to make monthly pledges to the Good Shepherd Orphanage in Vietnam. It was through this group that I first met Carol.

Carol had been Lauri's neighbor. She often mused that Lauri was everything she wasn't . . . independent, free-thinking, atheist, and braless. Yet Carol, with her conservative

Christian upbringing, was drawn to become her friend. Carol's own love for children and her desire to help them led her to join the group as well. She and I had recognized a kindred spirit in each other as soon as we'd met.

Now worry reflected in Carol's eyes as she broke the silence. "No matter what they say we will not carry money to Vietnam," she said emphatically.

To me the idea that we would even be asked to seemed farfetched. That was the least of my worries.

Cheryl Markson and "the other Carol," Carol Westlake, met us at the gate at Stapleton International Airport in Denver as planned. It was the state of their appearances that surprised me. When I met them at the Friends of Children of Vietnam convention two months earlier, both women were professionally and smartly dressed. But now they were haggard, their eyes puffy and tired-looking, their hair barely combed, their clothes crumpled. Cheryl explained that they had been working day and night to complete paperwork for hundreds of adoptions before Saigon fell.

Both women had adopted children through FCVN. I had met the Marksons' two birth children and their three adopted ones at their home in February. I could understand how this personal experience fueled their devotion to the agency—as well as to the children who still waited in Vietnam.

Cheryl held out a large blue duffel bag. "These are completed dossiers to be taken to Saigon. Don't let them out of your sight. Cherie will need these to assign homes to the remaining orphans." Her serious expression impressed me with the importance of the bag. Then she winked. "Take good care of these, LeAnn. Your paperwork is in here too."

I could feel my face flushing with excitement. Carol and I looked at each other, both grinning like exuberant children. I was one step closer to having a son. With our dossier in Saigon, he could be with us by the end of the year. I eagerly reached for the bag and almost dropped it. It felt as if it were made of lead although quite the opposite was true. It held nearly forty pounds of adoptive parents' hopes and dreams.

Still giddy, I turned back to hear more instructions. The prospect of adopting a son increased my confidence and determination. Then, just as if Carol had been looking into a crystal ball on the plane, her intuition became reality.

Cheryl was holding out a bundle of cash to be carried to Saigon. Carol was slowly and deliberately shaking her head back and forth. How had she known?

"There's $10,000 here," Cheryl pleaded. "Eight thousand in cash and $2,000 in money orders. The Vietnamese currency is so unstable now it's nearly useless. With these American dollars, Cherie will be able to buy out an entire commissary for the orphans." I could see Carol still wasn't convinced.

"Listen," Cheryl said, "without this money, the children might go hungry. They will certainly go without medicine."

The impact of those words hit me hard. I took the cash.

Of course I did.

I didn't know if I was being brave or stupid, but there didn't seem to be any other choice.

By the expression on her face, I knew Carol was quite sure I was being stupid. Cheryl must have noticed too, and attempted to ease her worry by telling us to simply hand the money over if we were mugged on our way to Saigon.

The appalled look on Carol's face told me she did not find that statement particularly reassuring.

"Sometimes there are hijackers in Vietnam," Cheryl warned. "Sometimes people in authority will confiscate your money for what they claim to be official reasons. It wasn't always like that. These are desperate times in Vietnam and the people are becoming desperate too. Some try to get money any way they can to prepare for their family's survival or escape."

"I'm sure we'll be fine," I predicted as we exchanged hugs and good-byes. We made our way to the restroom, with Carol telling me how foolish I was being and listing all the things that could happen to us if I smuggled money into

Saigon. Though I found her warnings irritating, I tried to be patient with her cautious approach to life. A part of me even admired it.

"I'm not worried," I assured her as I slipped into a stall to hide the cash in my bra.

The difficulties of getting visas and flight plans paled before the task of making $10,000 simulate the shape of a woman's body. Initially, I just stuck the bundles into my bra and looked down at the lumpy contour. The hard edges of the bundles would be obvious at fifty paces. In high school I had always wished for a bigger bra size, but now a 36D would have proved invaluable for more reasons than I had thought then.

"I'm not sure I can fit all this into a 32B," I called to Carol who waited outside the stall.

It was strange how this valuable paper could quickly be reduced to a problem of shape.

"How's it going?" Carol asked, hearing my chuckles.

"It looks like I stuffed my bra with Kleenex and forgot to take them out of the box!"

Her reply was lost as I removed the bundles of money and took handfuls of bills from them. I fit them into layers in the bra, flattening it out here, thickening the layers there. Green cash stuck out everywhere as I tried to arrange it into a shape similar to human anatomy. I slipped back into my shirt and opened the stall door to show Carol the finished look. Hands on my hips, I strutted past her and did a quick twirl, my face wearing its most seductive pout. I could have put Dolly Parton to shame.

Carol's eyes widened and she burst out laughing. The surprise on her face sent me into a fit of giggles. People around us stared, smiled, and moved on as we howled until tears streamed down our faces. We were bent over double, holding our sides, unable to stop though our ribs were aching. When the laughter threatened to relinquish its hold on us, all I had to do was stand up and we collapsed into hilarity again.

24

Chapter Two

When we finally caught our breath, the tension had dissipated and we were strengthened in our friendship and ready for whatever lay ahead.

At least I thought we were ready.

When we boarded the plane for San Francisco, the flight attendant and I debated whether the duffel bag could be carried on board. I could still hear Cheryl telling me not to let it out of my sight. After a short explanation, she relented and I put the bag on the floor in front of my seat and used it as a footrest. It was probably against regulations, but I didn't care. There was no way I was going to separate myself from the paperwork which brought us closer to our son, a son I wanted so badly and could only anticipate holding in my arms.

It was only the third time I had flown so I gawked out the window as we flew over the Rocky Mountains and then crossed far above the desert. I smiled as I looked at my best friend beside me. What on earth did we think we were doing? We hardly fit the picture of daring crusaders. Because I was smaller than my seven siblings, my brothers had nicknamed me Scrub, a term used for the runt of the litter of pigs. I resented being referred to as "skinny" and preferred the term "petite." With my short brown hair and hazel eyes, I had sometimes been described as being "cute" and on a good day, maybe even "attractive." But Carol was beautiful. She measured five feet tall, with dark-brown hair to her shoulders, gorgeous brown eyes, and a covergirl complexion. She seemed tense as she leaned back in her seat.

I couldn't seem to relax either. I kept remembering the fearful expression on Mark's face when I left him and I felt guilty and sad that I was making him so unhappy. When I voiced these emotions to Carol, she confided that her thoughts had been following similar paths. She was not only sad about leaving her family, but still uncertain of the wisdom of going to Vietnam at all.

She had arranged for us to spend the night with her sister Suzanne in San Francisco. She warned me that since the war had escalated Suzanne had withdrawn her support of our plans and would certainly try to talk us out of going.

I could see from her strained expression that she wasn't ready to face this new challenge. What if she lost her courage and changed her mind about going with me? As I considered this I realized that, although I didn't know how I would manage, there was no way I'd turn back now.

I tried to evoke the magic words that had so far helped us settle our fears.

"We'll be fine," I said. "We'll be fine." Carol smiled.

It helped our moods when, after landing in San Francisco, two good-looking men tried to pick us up. We accepted their offer to carry our heavy bags to the locker area and listened to their extravagant claims about the fun we'd have together as they showed us the town. Then we told them we weren't interested.

"Thanks for carrying our luggage though," we added, pretending to be gracious. They weren't impressed as they scowled off.

A quick trip to the bathroom and I was flat chested again. My skin had become hot and sweaty under that expensive padding. We stowed the money and the duffel bag in a locker and then, with lighter steps, went to meet Carol's sister.

Suzanne was a beautiful, independent Bay-area physician. Carol admitted privately that she couldn't understand why Suzanne's approval had always been especially important to her. She warned me that the evening ahead might be difficult.

Suzanne was waiting near the airport's outer doors, petite and fashionably dressed. Her lips were pursed and her dark eyes flashed as we approached. Carol hugged her and then introduced me.

"Hello." Suzanne was curt, barely acknowledging me. It was my first inkling that perhaps I hadn't taken Carol's warning seriously enough. This was not going to be easy.

Chapter Two

We picked up our bags and followed Suzanne through the sliding glass doors to her car parked right outside. As we loaded the bags into the trunk, Carol, probably searching for some way to ease the tension, blundered blithely into our first war zone.

"It's hard to believe that in just twenty-four hours we'll be here again, ready to leave for Saigon."

"We'll see about that!" Suzanne snapped, biting off each syllable. Carol looked at me and rolled her eyes.

Nervously, we crawled into the car. The stress was heightened by the smell of exhaust, the voice on the loud speaker, and the congestion of people and traffic. A policeman signaled us to move quickly out of the area. The intimidation seemed to increase for Carol inside the car, perhaps because we were on Suzanne's turf.

Suzanne broke the awkward silence to declare a truce. "We're going to have a nice dinner before we talk about this," she said bluntly.

We dined in a lovely restaurant with wonderful food and wine but Carol ate very little. I sensed the shrimp and steak were going down her throat like walnuts. Small talk eased the tension only a bit.

The drive through the suburb to the condominium was beautiful at sunset. *This isn't so bad,* I thought, *we're getting along pretty well.* As we entered her condo I was impressed with the high sloping ceilings, lush green plants, and lovely furnishings. I turned with a smile to compliment Suzanne, but the stern look on her face told me the truce had ended.

She closed the door behind us and the battle was on in earnest.

Carol, already fearful and indecisive, was no match for Suzanne's determination to save her sister from what she saw as a foolish and dangerous journey. Although Carol and I both pleaded for the necessity of bringing out children before the government collapsed, Suzanne would have nothing of that argument.

"I just want you to see the other side of the story," she said. "You are two naive housewives from Middle America risking your lives. You have no idea what you're getting into. Everything is getting worse there day by day."

"I call the State Department every single day," Carol retorted. "They keep saying it's okay to go. The more children you can get out the better, they tell us."

"Of course they're going to say that! Carol, you have your own sons who need you. What if you get killed?" She threw her hands up in frustration.

I tried to point out that we felt compelled to go, knowing that someone would soon have to bring my son out, perhaps in an even more dangerous situation.

"It's just not safe!" she said raising her voice a pitch. "It's ridiculous to go there now." Then in a low tone she added, "I'm scared for you, Carol. I love you."

The conversation seemed endless as she went on to list all the reasons we should not go. Each time I tried to explain why we should, Suzanne had a rebuttal.

She sat down next to Carol on the couch and stared into her eyes. "You just don't get it, Carol." Her voice shook. "I don't care what the State Department says. I don't care what LeAnn says. All I care about is you and I'm afraid I'm going to lose you." She stood and paced across the room. "I'll do anything to keep you from going. I'll lock you in the bathroom if I have to!"

I could see I was not about to change her mind. Besides, it was Carol's battle. I knew what I had to do. Somehow I felt Suzanne would never hear what I said anyway. She was too angry and worried to listen.

Realizing that, I declared that I was going to Vietnam no matter what she said and I went to bed in desperation. Suzanne's insistence that we not go was only strengthening my determination . . . until I lay alone in the darkness. I knew Suzanne was saying some of the things Mark wanted to say to me before I left. Part of me wanted to abandon this trip and run home to my family.

I could hear Carol and Suzanne talk far into the night. I listened as they called their parents in New York. Though they were less enthusiastic than before, they insisted the decision was Carol's to make. Having reached an impasse, Carol and her sister finally went to bed.

In the morning the battle continued. In her steadfast pursuit of a definite answer, Carol called the State Department one last time. I couldn't believe she was calling them again. What did she expect them to say? A part of her was disappointed that the message was the same.

"Get as many children out as possible," her contact urged.

I was losing perspective. I knew Carol was frightened and searching for something to make her feel secure in her decision to go, but I was tired of wrangling and I couldn't help her anymore.

We sat in uncomfortable silence trying to swallow the tea and toast.

"I won't be a party to endangering your lives," Suzanne told us in a matter-of-fact tone. "I'll drop you off at the nearest bus stop and you can catch a bus into San Francisco."

Carol and I just looked at each other. I was mad enough to walk to the airport dragging my bag behind me.

Once again we loaded our luggage into the trunk of Suzanne's car and she drove us to the bus stop a few blocks away. After we quietly took our bags from the car and placed them on the curb, she hugged Carol tightly.

"I hope you know what you are doing," she sighed. She ignored me and I couldn't help but feel she blamed me for getting her sister into this mess in the first place.

We watched as she drove away, leaving us alone on a curb in a big, strange city.

We caught the bus to downtown San Francisco and sat in utter stillness while it traveled up and down the beautiful hills. I felt I wasn't being a very good friend to Carol. I didn't know how to help her.

Finally she spoke.

"We didn't need this, that's for sure. I can understand why she's so worried about me, but I never thought it would be like this. Now I wish we'd left from Los Angeles instead."

I looked at her face, pale with worry. I didn't know what to say. She stared blankly out the window.

The sun shone so brightly on the palm trees. We had been advised to ride a cable car all day to see the sights of the city. Though our flight wasn't scheduled to depart until 6 P.M., I knew we were in no mood for sightseeing.

The clanging of a passing cable car put music in my heart and I smiled as I imagined Tony Bennett singing "I Left My Heart in San Francisco."

Mark sang that song.

We hailed a taxi for a short ride to the Vietnamese consulate to pick up our visas. We were told we would have to wait for an hour so we decided to try shopping in the big city. Lugging our suitcases, we made our way to a nearby department store to browse for a few minutes. I knew I was stressed when I couldn't enjoy shopping. We rode the elevator up to the restaurant where we ate lunch at a table decorated with cheerful daffodils. It was a nice distraction, but Carol was still looking for help.

"I think I should call Denver again to make sure the trip is still on, don't you?"

"Sure. And while you're at it, why don't you call the State Department," I teased, trying to lighten the mood. "I'm sure they're expecting another call from you. Maybe something has changed in the past few hours."

She managed a smile.

Her fear was contagious and even I was beginning to think that maybe it was too dangerous to go. As she headed for the pay phone, I secretly found myself hoping that we'd be advised to abandon our mission so this turmoil could be ended.

When Carol made her way back to the table, her eyes were still troubled. "They say everything is still on. Cheryl also said that Cherie had called from Saigon to say that Friends For All Children . . . you know, the other agency out of Denver . . . they're waiting for approval from the Ministry of the Interior to bring out 600 children and staff members," she read from her notes. "Cheryl says when we get there, we should ask Cherie to investigate and make a similar request if possible."

"What does that have to do with us?"

"Nothing, I imagine. They're just looking at future possibilities I think." We looked at each other for reassurance. "But it does sound like they're expecting things to get much worse."

"They're working to get their staff out while we're still working to get in." I looked down at my plate and picked at my food, clearly aware that it wasn't resting very well in my fluttering stomach.

Carol's soft voice broke the quiet which had settled over the table. "LeAnn, do you think we could be in a bit over our heads here?"

I had no answer.

I wished she'd quit asking.

We finished our lunch in quiet and gathered our bags to return to the consulate for our visas. The tiny room seemed crowded with the big mahogany desk, the elderly clerk, the two of us, and an American man and his Vietnamese wife. While we waited we talked with the couple who were trying to expedite the process of getting their children cleared to leave Vietnam. I asked what they knew about the status of things there.

"It's a very shaky situation," the man shook his head. "I can give you very little encouragement."

I wished I hadn't asked.

We started back to the bus station, stowing away our visas. Carol reminded me that she had promised to call Al before we left. We had four hours before our flight and even though I was sure it would be a mistake for her to call him, I kept

31

quiet. We stopped at a dilapidated phone booth near the bus station, set our luggage down, and Carol placed her call.

"Have you heard the news today?" he warned. "They're bombing closer to Saigon! If I had any say, you'd come home."

She shouted above the traffic, telling him we would leave Vietnam as quickly as possible.

She hung up the phone and began to weep, oblivious to the traffic and the staring eyes of passing pedestrians. I waited quietly by the bags until she felt ready to talk.

"He said to think about him and the kids. LeAnn, what am I going to do? All along he has encouraged me on this. But now he doesn't even support me!"

Slowly we continued our walk to the bus station. As we passed a newspaper stand, a headline jumped out at me. "War Rages Near Saigon City Limits." I moved between Carol and the newspaper stand, hoping she wouldn't see it, knowing that if she did, she might not make the journey. Selfishly, I didn't want her to go home.

She was still crying as we sat at the shabby chrome table at the bus station. She pulled a tissue from her purse, wiped the mascara stains from her face and said, "Maybe we should just go back to Iowa City."

There it was.

It was almost a relief that she'd finally spoken what I knew she was thinking. I had expected this moment and had rehearsed my response. I took a deep breath to fortify myself. "You have to do what's right for you, Carol, but I know I've got to go, even if it's alone."

She looked up with confusion and surprise. "But the war is so dangerous now, LeAnn. The whole thing has changed since we first said we'd go. Maybe we should just call Cheryl and tell her we've both changed our minds. Surely she'll understand."

Though her idea was tempting, I answered, "I'm going, Carol. I have to." I was almost ashamed at my obstinacy in the face of danger. But there was no way I could turn back now. And I was beginning to wonder, with Carol so frightened, if I might be better off without her. Yet I was afraid of all the unknowns by myself. Reaching across the table, I held her hand.

"I can't understand myself what's driving me to go, Carol. All I know is that I'm supposed to. And I know we'll be okay."

"Well, I could never let you go alone. I promised to go with you!"

"I can do it by myself," I whined through blubbering tears. Passersby pretended not to notice.

"No. I'm going with you," she said with an almost angry determination.

"We'll be fine." I tried to revive the old magic.

Carol tried to smile and took a deep breath. "We will," she said firmly then added with a little laugh, "I've made my last phone call. There's no one else to face."

I felt enough courage for both of us as we boarded the transit bus for the airport. There we went immediately to the locker and were relieved to find the duffel bag and money still safely stored. After a quick trip to the woman's room where I reestablished my $10,000 bra, we proceeded to check our baggage.

The ticket agent seemed annoyed as he issued the free tickets generously donated by the airline. Finally he blurted out that he resented our traveling to a foreign country to help orphans when there were so many American children in need.

That argument had always annoyed me.

"And what are *you* doing to help the American children?" I challenged. He confessed that he didn't assist personally but felt that *we* should instead of traveling abroad to help those in a foreign land. I debated his thinking which I always found illogical.

He went on to describe the plight of the American Indians and tried to chastise us for not "staying home and helping our own."

"What difference does it make what country orphans are from?" I argued. "What does geography have to do with it? Poverty and starvation know no boundaries. Shouldn't we help everyone in need, regardless of race or location?"

"Spoken like a true crusader," Carol interjected and I realized I had been shouting from my soapbox.

"LeAnn Thieman, please call the airport operator," came the page.

My heart stopped, then raced madly.

Who could possibly need me? I was certain it only meant trouble. My mind anxiously flashed to my girls and I wondered if they were all right.

As I went to grab my tickets from the agent, he held on to them momentarily then looked into my face as he released them.

"I see your point," he said somewhat humbly. "What you're doing is right. I wish you the best of luck . . . really."

I smiled. "Sorry to be so preachy. All this isn't easy for me," I stammered as I rushed off to find the airport phone.

I was relieved when the caller identified herself as a California chapter representative telling me where to meet her in the terminal. She had packages to be taken to Saigon. When we met her at the baggage check and I recognized her as Barbara Wong, whom I had met at the FCVN convention.

"Will they let us check all this?" I asked, staring at the eighteen boxes at her feet.

"We do it all the time," she reassured me. "The airlines are great. They make exceptions to the rules for us. They haul equipment and packages to Vietnam all the time and never charge us. Their employees even serve as escorts for kids when we need them. Sometimes when FCVN can't get through by phone to Vietnam, the airlines let us use their communication lines."

Chapter Two

Still, as we loaded our cargo onto the baggage check-in counter, I felt a little ridiculous.

But by then the whole world seemed ridiculous.

"One of the babies you'll bring out will likely be the daughter we've been waiting for." Barbara's face was luminescent as she showed us a snapshot of the baby girl assigned to them. Suddenly this mission was developing a more personal flavor and my excitement grew.

So with nearly two dozen pieces of baggage checked and $10,000 in my bra, we boarded the 747 for Hawaii.

Chapter Three

The mammoth interior of the plane seemed a little frightening to me as we sat down and fastened our seat belts. We felt like two country girls embarking on a big-city adventure. Carol sat next to the window and looked out as men maneuvered their carts and placed baggage on conveyor belts. "I wonder if we'll ever see our luggage again."

Seeing all the tourists in their bright colored shirts spurred my enthusiasm.

"They're probably on their way to lie on the beach," I said wistfully. "I've always dreamed of going to Hawaii, but never imagined it would be on my way to Saigon."

"Do you think it's significant that it's April Fools Day?" Carol teased.

Were we being fools? I couldn't help but wonder as I felt the plane pull off the runway.

Putting on the earphones, we rested our heads back against the seats, listening to music while thumbing through the Pan American Airlines Magazine. Carol nudged me as she traced the course of flight along the map with her finger from California to Saigon. We both smiled in an attempt to bolster one another's confidence.

We sat without talking for a while. Then Carol took her earphones off and I did the same. She talked about how she wanted to be strong and excited but was unable to get past her fear. She gazed out the window.

"I always play this little game while flying. I pretend to be a soaring seagull. Being so high in the sky I believe I have easier access to God. The sense of freedom is usually exhilarating. But today it's scary." I gave her hand a little squeeze, again not knowing what to say. She continued to stare with intensity out the window. Like she was looking for something. Maybe for an answer that wasn't there.

The six-hour trip went by quickly. During the one-hour layover in Hawaii, we walked outside awhile. The beautiful flowers, red, pink, yellow, and white all with lush greenery, made the air fragrant. The fresh ocean breeze almost tasted salty.

"Not to say I don't like you, Carol," I joshed, "but I wish Mark were here and we were going on the honeymoon we never had."

Carol laughed. "I feel like such a pain in the neck, I don't blame you!" She admitted her brief respite from fear was giving way to a persistent gnawing in her stomach. She ordered ice cream in the airport restaurant.

"I see the stress isn't squelching your appetite!" she quipped sarcastically while she watched me scarf down a huge sandwich, fries, and a malt.

It was eerie boarding the plane again, enroute to Guam, and realizing that where hundreds had been sitting earlier, only a dozen people remained.

"Obviously the flight to Saigon is not a popular one," I joked, not really finding it very funny. "Why are they using such a big plane to take so few people?"

The flight attendant overheard and answered that the plane would be filled to capacity when it left Saigon.

The fact that we were headed for a country that everyone else was anxious to leave tormented me as I sprawled out over several seats and tried to sleep.

Carol sat upright staring out into the darkness.

Chapter Three

I woke to the sound of my friend retching. I immediately sat up. "Carol, what's wrong?" Only then I realized the tremendous effect this struggle was having on her.

"I feel awful." She looked awful too. Her face was pale and clammy. Her sunken eyes reflected the pain she could no longer suppress. I was torn. A part of me wanted to encourage her, hoping to help her gain confidence, while another part of me was afraid to push her into doing something that would make her more sick.

"Maybe we should turn back," Carol mumbled. "What if I get to Vietnam and get worse?"

I was so confused.

How should I help her?

The fog of my sleep clouded my mind and worry set it racing. What if she becomes more ill? What would happen to her then? And where would she be when illness struck?

For what might have been the first time on our trip, I tried to put my own intentions aside as I considered what would be best for her.

"I think you should consider getting off in Guam to get medical care and go back to the States as soon as possible," I said softly, holding her cold, sweaty hand.

"Wouldn't you come with me?" her voice and eyes pleaded.

I paused as if to contemplate my response, but the answer was clear in my mind.

"I don't know if I'm strong or just stubborn, Carol, but I know I have to go on to Saigon."

She moaned and laid her head back on the pillow.

I couldn't go back to sleep. My thoughts were scrambled as I tried to consider what would be the right thing to do. My head told me to call off the trip and go home with her, where she would get medical treatment. But my heart insisted I should go on.

Eight long hours later, we arrived in Guam. We were allowed to get off the plane, but since it would have taken an hour to get through security and into the U.S. base there, we just stood on the runway hoping to get some fresh air. But the night air was oppressive and heat seemed to radiate up from the pavement. American soldiers stood nearby, their uniforms clinging to them, sweat dripping from their foreheads.

"And I thought Iowa summers were hot and humid!" I cajoled, trying to ease the tension. Carol smiled. We stood in silence. I watched her stare at the terminal. Would she stay in Guam?

When the time came to board, I quietly went back in and sat down. She followed.

Her decision had been made.

The plane remained sparsely filled. As the attendants gave safety instructions for the flight in several languages, I nodded knowingly as if to understand them all, but Carol could not smile at my joking.

Pillows and blankets were passed out. I leaned back and closed my eyes, still worried about Carol.

"How can you sleep at a time like this?" she muttered. She reclined back in her seat with her face against the small white pillow. Her eyes were wide open. "Everyone else is sleeping," she whispered. "It's an international flight. I should be excited but I'm just scared."

"How can I help you?" I whispered back.

"I don't know. I know I have to find strength within myself."

A young flight attendant made rounds checking on the passengers. He crouched beside Carol's seat. "How ya doing?" he asked. His dark-brown curly hair was rumpled as if he might have been sleeping. To my amazement, Carol began to give a truthful, detailed answer to his question. He stayed down on his haunches and listened carefully as she talked. What was it about him that allowed her to verbalize her thoughts so freely?

"I'm just so immobilized by my fear and I want so badly

to be strong," she said.

"Why are you so afraid?" he coaxed softly.

"I'm afraid I may be making one of the biggest mistakes of my life. The war is getting worse all the time." She ended the sentence abruptly.

His voice was barely audible. "Are you afraid you won't come back?"

"Maybe," she blurted through tears. "I could die there! Or what if I just get sicker? What'll happen to me then? What will happen to my kids?"

His gentle brown eyes showed genuine concern as he listened, his hand resting on hers.

"At first my entire family said I should go . . . my parents, my sister, my husband. Their advice has always been really important to me. That made my decision then much easier. But in the past few days they've all changed their minds." Her voice broke. "Now they're all telling me not to go. Do you know how hard it is to do something that everybody you love disapproves of? I'm beginning to wonder if I'm selfish."

"Selfish? Hardly. I think what you are doing is one of the most generous things I can imagine."

She smiled and shook her head slowly. "It's always been important to me to do what's right. And now I'm feeling like this might be all wrong."

"How can helping orphans be wrong?"

She shrugged. "I'm feeling like such a coward."

"On the contrary, I think you're showing incredible courage to have continued on this trip in spite of everything telling you not to."

"He's right," I chimed in. "Think about it, Carol. You've shown more courage than I have. If my family had spoken up like yours did, I wonder if I would have had the guts to go."

Then with a note of enthusiasm the flight attendant said, "Tell me more about why you wanted to go in the first place, Carol."

She took a deep breath and a grin crossed her lips as she

recited the litany of reasons that compelled her to volunteer.

"Wow, this is an opportunity of a lifetime, isn't it?" His face lit with a smile. "Rarely do people have a chance to do something so directly for humanity. You'll be changing lives forever!"

Then he stood, stating this was his last flight for Pan American Airlines. He gave Carol's hand a final squeeze. "You can do this. If you want to be strong, you will be. Just believe it." With a wink, he walked back to his quarters.

We never saw him again.

Carol sat quietly. I nestled my head into the pillow and dozed.

When I woke, Carol was just returning to her seat. Her hair was pulled back in a twist, her makeup applied beautifully.

"I'm better!" she announced almost smugly.

"What?" I sat up, hardly believing my eyes and ears.

"LeAnn, I can't exactly explain this, but I'm okay and I'm going to Saigon. Since talking with the steward, I know we will be fine," she said with an incandescent smile.

"Are you sure?" I was skeptical of the sudden change in her — yet she seemed more relaxed and confident than I had ever seen her.

"I'm sure," she said positively.

"What did he say that you hadn't heard before?"

"I don't know!" she almost giggled. "All of a sudden I knew I had the power to be strong. He was like a guardian angel."

I breathed a sigh of relief and put my arms around her. I could hardly fathom the change in her, yet I could relate to the feeling of transformation as I remembered what happened to me on Easter Sunday.

We both reclined across several seats and tried to sleep, this time filled with renewed hope and excitement.

Chapter Four

"President Thieu is dead, you know," a third American said as he moved from his stool to one closer to our conversation in the Manila airport. Though he claimed to be a U.S. government employee, and therefore privy to inside information, the other men protested in disbelief. I sipped my bottled cola and looked from one stranger's face to the next.

I didn't know what to believe anymore.

"He was shot by a rebel last week. If he's not dead, he's in critical condition."

When I joined the others in challenging his report, he asked if I'd seen any television coverage of the Vietnamese president recently. I admitted I had not and he triumphantly rested his case.

There were less than a dozen people in the dim airport lounge, all gathered now at the old-fashioned wooden bar and stools. The cheaply made chrome tables and chairs sat empty behind us. We listened as one man told of his efforts to raise enough money to get his Vietnamese wife and children out of the country before it fell. Perhaps it was his need for hope that argued with the man who predicted the country's imminent doom. A chubby bald man added a positive note as he applauded Carol and me for our humanitarian efforts and assured us we'd be safe.

We were the only women there, and each of the men took a turn advising us not to drink the water or eat fresh foods, where to stay, and what to see. Though there was an air of lightheartedness, caution was the prevailing message. All our advisers agreed that the country would not fall for at least a year.

A new Carol seemed to listen and respond to their words. There was an excited confidence about her that seemed genuine. I was relieved as I didn't know how much longer I could have mustered enough courage for both of us.

As Carol and I compared notes with our fellow passengers, a young soldier in military khakis entered smartly.

"The tour bus is ready," he announced. Airport officials had been reluctant to admit the reason for our extended layover in Manila. Instead they offered us a tour of their city. Several of the men declined the invitation but Carol and I decided to take advantage of the opportunity. With our fears resolved, we were feeling happy and anxious to be tourists until our Saigon mission began. Before we boarded, the two officers confiscated our passports. Carol and I shrugged at each other. There seemed to be no alternative than to trust we'd get them back.

A half dozen of us climbed onto a shabby old white bus. Carol and I chose one of the less rickety-looking benches and managed a joke about lugging around the precious forty-pound satchel placed safely at my feet.

Manila's modern architecture and high-rise buildings looked like a scene from an American city, but the streets, congested with Asian pedestrians and bicycles, reminded me that I was not in my native land. Open-air buses painted bright, wild colors seemed out of place in this part of the world. The U.S. left many of them behind after World War II, the guide explained, and now it was popular to paint the jeep-like buses, called jitneys, in bold designs of dragons and flowers. Like all the vehicles in the traffic, they were over-loaded with people.

Chapter Four

We passed the site where Douglas MacArthur said, "I shall return."

"I can't believe we're really here," I said, and Carol smiled. It was a relief that we could start to enjoy our very unexpected world travels.

The guide announced we were approaching the Manila Cemetery and Memorial, where over 17,000 U.S. military personnel from World War II were buried. When we neared the cemetery we both felt a sobering awareness of our surroundings. Most of the dead, the guide said, lost their lives in the defense of the Philippines. We climbed out of the bus with me still toting the satchel. As far as our eyes could see there were rows and rows of white marble cross headstones on the meticulously groomed lush green landscape. We walked quietly thinking about all the suffering represented there.

Carol talked about her brother, Gerry, who served in the Marines in Vietnam at Da Nang. She wondered what he had seen and experienced. She felt thankful he was alive.

I thought about the men and women already killed in Vietnam. How many more died in other countries and other wars? Would a similar tribute be made to those killed in Vietnam? I uttered a brief prayer of gratitude that my brother, Denny, who served in Vietnam, was not among them. He lost his right arm in the war. Seeing the thousands of crosses made me newly grateful he had not lost his life.

A blanket of sadness draped over our little group as we approached the memorial and read the inscription: "In proud remembrance of the achievements of her sons and in humble tribute to their sacrifices this memorial has been erected by the United States of America 1941–1945." Our grief intensified as we saw that the ten walls listed names of over 36,000 missing in action.

For the first time in my life I realized the true cost of war.

My arms were tired from carrying the duffel bag so Carol took it while we finished the walking tour.

"I'm tired from lack of sleep and slightly queasy from not eating," Carol admitted, "but I'm feeling better than I have since leaving Iowa." She radiated a smile. "For the first time I feel like we're really united on this!"

From there we returned to the airport. We were relieved when the officer handed back our passports.

"You'd better hurry and rejoin your group," he said.

The flight was boarding for Saigon.

Chapter Five

Sunshine filled the plane's cabin as the flight continued to Saigon. I could hardly believe the change in Carol. Her enthusiasm bolstered mine instead of draining it as before. It seemed a bit too coincidental that the flight attendant had made one final flight on which he'd been able to offer Carol the exact inspiration she needed. Maybe he was an angel.

As the Pan Am jet approached Saigon, we leaned to look out the window at the flat, brown terrain below.

"This is it!" Carol beamed. "It wasn't easy, but we're here!"

Our enthusiasm was quickly tempered as the airport came into view.

I hadn't fully understood we were entering a war zone until the plane touched down at Tan Son Nhut airport. Unlike other international airports we'd seen on the trip, this runway was lined with aircraft painted the olive greens, tans, and black of jungle camouflage. The run-down, unpainted airport buildings looked more like the deserted, decaying buildings scattered across our familiar Iowa farmland than like a commercial airline facility.

The somewhat comical pickup attempt by a middle-aged man on the flight had Carol and me giggling as we stepped off the plane.

"You must be tired after such a long trip," he told her slyly. "Come to my house and lie down."

Carol stifled a laugh as she declined his offer.

"The Saigon seduction," I teased as I hummed the theme song from a popular soap opera.

But our laughter ended abruptly as we descended the steps into the sweltering heat of Vietnam.

We crossed the sunbaked pavement toward what passed for a customs building. I looked down to check my appearance when I saw the soldiers waiting to check us through the baggage claim. Every nerve in my body was jumping. In Denver, Cheryl had told me to keep quiet and "just act natural." She'd also told us that we could buy anything or anyone in Vietnam, even our way through customs, so we both carried cash in our purses. I was most afraid they'd take one look at me and know that this voluptuous figure was not an act of nature. My heart began to thump heavily under all that cash.

We followed the bare, grimy, two-by-four railings, stained by thousands of sweaty hands before ours, toward the counter where the Vietnamese soldiers waited for us. They seemed annoyed with our eighteen boxes of supplies already stacked before them. Would they open them all? When I lifted my bags onto the counter, I just knew they were about to arrest me for smuggling. One barked at me in Vietnamese, gesturing to the bags. I explained they contained clothing and documents. When they didn't seem to understand, I shouted. Somehow, I was sure they'd understand English better if I raised the decibel level. Perhaps more importantly, the shouting vented some of the pressure I was feeling. Unfortunately, my experience with Asian men in military uniforms was limited to John Wayne World War II movies—in which they were the bad guys. I knew these were the '70s, and this was Vietnam, but I was way out of my element. I was trembling, trying not to let my fear show.

Then I knew we were in trouble. The soldier's eyes began to move very slowly over us. Oh, no! Something had given me away. What would they do to us when they discovered the cash?

His eyes stared fiercely. I thought his face would shatter when suddenly he smiled flirtatiously at Carol. "Pretty," he told her, his English perfect, for this business at least.

"Thank you," she responded primly. Thank goodness for her tact.

The soldiers muttered over the bags and boxes one by one, stacking them on the floor at the end of their counter. One of them grunted as he lifted the forty-pound duffel bag, then unzipped it and looked inside. Shrugging, he waved us on. Hardly daring to make eye contact, Carol and I picked up our bags and steeled ourselves for our next trial. We followed the other passengers being directed through the makeshift passageway and finally to the exit.

We made it!

We were in Saigon. Now all we had to do was take care of our business and go home.

We stood at the doorway surprised and relieved, wondering what to do next.

"LeAnn! LeAnn!"

I turned to see Cherie Clark waving to us. Still operating on the adrenalin from the customs check, I rushed to hug her. I had met her at the convention in February, and it was great to see her familiar face. As I stepped back I noticed her small frame looked worn and frazzled, as though she hadn't slept in days.

The first words out of her mouth made it clear that our mission had changed since we boarded the plane in San Francisco.

"Did you hear the news?" Her haggard face lit up with excitement. I realized then that we'd been traveling for over twenty-four hours and had no exposure to television, radio, or newspapers.

"President Ford has okayed a giant babylift! Instead of taking out a half dozen babies, you're going to help take out nearly 200 . . . if we're lucky!"

Two hundred babies! Carol and I looked at each other, smiles illuminating faces.

This was our true mission!

That compelling, unexplainable compulsion to go — the questions about what could possibly make us fly into a war zone — were suddenly crystal clear.

We *were* supposed to come!

Carol and I stammered with excitement.

We tried to comprehend her message while we followed her to customs to get all the boxes. As we loaded them in the car, she continued her story. She told us her husband, Tom, had left the night before with fifty-seven children on a cargo plane bound for the United States. New excitement temporarily overshadowed her exhaustion as she spoke with pride of the evacuation. World Airways president Edward Daly, sympathetic to the orphan cause, had supplied them with a plane and within one hour the children were out of Saigon. But there were still hundreds more to be evacuated.

With bags and eighteen boxes packed around us and on top of the Volkswagon bug, the three of us jammed into the front bucket seats and headed for the orphanage.

Cherie confidently drove the rickety VW through the two-lane streets crowded with six to eight lanes of traffic. She maneuvered the car around hundreds of bicycles, Hondas, and pushcarts loaded with people and their possessions. Horns honked, tires screeched, people yelled as the car veered through the congested chaos.

I gawked trying to take in sights, so foreign, so exciting. The hot, humid air was permeated with the smell of fish and fowl. Street vendors lined the sidewalks to sell uncovered meats and vegetables. I winced as I watched flies swarming around the plucked chicken carcasses hanging from a wire rack. Their heads and feet still intact, they were suspended from a rusty rod. Several live chickens were crowded into a small wire cage apparently awaiting the butcher's knife. The bare, rough wooden tables were covered with papers, soggy with the drainage from the produce they held. Signs in oriental script advertised the goods to passersby.

Even the deafening noises were unfamiliar to me as the citizens shouted to one another and loaded down bicycles and motor bikes buzzed by. It seemed thousands of Saigonese crowded the streets and sidewalks. Most of them were dressed alike in sandals, black pants, and white or black tunic tops. Though many women wore scarves as head coverings, it seemed that straw hats were worn by everyone. Men and women alike carried yokes on their shoulders with baskets or bags at both ends. I felt like I was part of a picture from *National Geographic* magazine.

Some buildings of tin and shabby wood barely seemed strong enough to stand. Others were modern and resembled those of concrete and brick in the States.

"This must be what they mean by culture shock," I said softly to Carol.

She commented about the unsightly new surroundings and we were surprised to hear Cherie quickly speak in defense of the city she'd come to love.

"This isn't the best part of the city. There are sections with magnificent buildings and houses as well as beautiful beaches and palm trees. This is like an island paradise. This is my home." Pride crept into her voice as she tried to help us see what she saw in Saigon.

She had left her home in Illinois two years before to help the innocent orphans of war. Originally she was an FCVN chapter president, nurse, and homemaker, just like me. She too had been asked to serve as an escort for children from Vietnam to the U.S. But unlike me, she had been able to bring back her own two adopted children, Johanna and Tahn. I only had to look around to understand the need that drew her to return to this country wracked with suffering. Her husband, Tom, an engineer with IBM, had taken a leave of absence from his work to accompany her and their seven

51

children to this land of need.

We passed a crowd shouting and shoving in front of a large building on one street corner. "That's the bank. Lots of businessmen are transferring piasters from Vietnamese banks to local branches of U.S. banks hoping the money will be safer when the communists come." Carol's and my eyes met and we cringed in unison. "Unfortunately, the banks run out of cash sometimes when too many come to withdraw their money. Occasionally it turns into a riot and people get hurt." She glanced at the camera I was pulling from my bag. "I wouldn't do that. You could be arrested. The police don't like people taking pictures of this."

Feeling somewhat embarrassed by my tourist-like behavior, I sheepishly put the camera away.

Kindly, Cherie said, "Remember, you're not in America anymore."

That was for sure.

Chapter Six

We turned onto a quieter, narrower side street and then pulled through the black, cast-iron gates past the high, fortified concrete walls of the Giah Dinh Center. The buildings we'd passed around it were dilapidated, two-story, gray, ramshackle homes with rusty, sloping roofs and boarded windows. Open trash cans had dotted the streets. In contrast, the center was stately and impressive. We pulled into the large circular drive at the entrance. Bright green trees, tall palms, and other foliage surrounded the area along with varieties of pink, yellow, and orange flowers. A large, two-story structure, the Center was built with blocks of smooth, white stone. Verandas edged with black iron railings crossed the outside of the second floor. Latticed bars decorated the windows. It resembled a mansion in New Orleans, the same French flavor creating a bit of elegance in the midst of squalor.

The car halted in the driveway in front of the entrance to the main building and immediately Vietnamese workers came from inside to help with the unloading of the boxes.

Inside I was thrilled to see Sister Therese, a Catholic nun whom I had also met at the FCVN convention. Her Michigan-based order had approved the request for her and her coworker, Sister Nancy, to direct FCVN's Thu Duc Center for toddlers and older children. Sister Nancy, a Montessori teacher, had left on the flight the night before. Sister Therese had wavy brown hair and a lighthearted smile. Unlike the nuns I had known as a child, she was dressed as casually as the rest of us.

"Look what I've got!" I announced as I reached into my blouse and under my bra. The nun's eyes widened. I pulled out the cash and money orders.

"My mom always said I should pin some cash to my bra for emergency money when I travel."

Laughter filled the room as Cherie took the emerging handfuls of money and placed them in the huge safe sitting in the corner. She thanked us for the risk we had taken and told us about the lifesaving supplies which could be purchased.

As Cherie closed the safe, a beautiful Vietnamese woman entered the room. She was introduced as Thuy, a social worker for FCVN who had studied as an exchange student at the University of Minnesota. She wore pants and a blouse with her waist-length brown hair tied back in a ribbon. Her broad smile welcomed us as she spoke perfect English. Her smile dimmed, though, and she told us there was already concern about whether she and her two adopted children would be allowed to leave Saigon with the rest of the staff when the time came.

Before Cherie could take us on a tour of the Center, Ross Meador came bounding into the office, excited about the news of the airlift. A young Californian, just twenty years old, with unkempt curly brown hair, a bushy mustache, and sweat-stained clothes, he had postponed college to volunteer time and energy to the orphans for the past eighteen months. He shook our hands feverishly and pushed his glasses back onto the bridge of his nose. I liked him immediately.

"Let me show you around," Cherie said. The outer office we were in was filled with two desks, out-of-date chairs, and a large rattan couch with flowered cushions. Stacks of files and papers gave a sense of disarray. A large ceiling fan attempted to move the hot, muggy air.

"We're bringing in children from the foster homes for the airlift. Here's the nursery," Cherie said as we passed through the heavy, wooden door. My years of working in a newborn nursery and pediatrics could not prepare me for the scene before me. The walls were lined with cribs, and mats covered the tile floors. On every mat there were several babies sleeping, crying, cooing. Some of the babies looked beautifully healthy. Others were deformed or sickly. Nursery smells of wet and dirty diapers, vomit, baby powder, and formula were multiplied tenfold in the hot, humid room. Though overcrowded, the room was meticulously clean. There were forty-five babies in an area that was meant to hold only ten infants too ill to be in the foster homes.

When FCVN had first been established in Vietnam, the children were cared for in a central location, an orphanage in another part of Saigon. After a measles outbreak had become an epidemic and many young lives were lost, the foster home project was instigated. Ads were put in local newspapers asking for breast-feeding women to care for babies. Breast milk provided the infant not only with nutrition but disease-resisting antibodies so desperately needed. Having someone to hold them and love them was equally important. The infants were visited weekly and their needs assessed by a social worker and medical team. It had proven to be an ideal program. Now the babies were coming in from these homes in preparation for their flights to freedom.

A large, wooden table in the center of the room, stocked with baby care items and surrounded by straight, wooden chairs, provided a work area. Six local women were caring for the babies. They were small and pretty with their long, black hair pulled back in barrettes. Each wore a plain but brightly colored yellow, pink, or blue smock. They looked up from their work to greet us with a smile. I knew another of FCVN's contributions there was the training of local workers. Dozens had benefited from the free programs teaching nutrition, hygiene, and childcare.

"They care for these babies as if they were their own," Cherie said affectionately. "They really love them. Normally they work twelve-hour shifts, but they've worked night and day since we learned about the airlift. They lie on the mats with the babies to sleep, then continue to work. I don't know what we'd do without them."

She gestured toward an alcove at the end of the room. "We even have a nursery." I gazed into the spotless white room, surprised to see four Isolettes housing four tiny infants.

"How did you get those here?" I asked in amazement.

"The airlines shipped them free. Cheryl brought two with her when she came in February." She introduced us to Kieu, a Vietnamese nurse working over one of the frail babies. "The Isolettes and Kieu have saved many lives," she said gently patting the woman's back. The nurse looked up with a smile then continued her work. "Dr. Cuong makes rounds twice a day so these babies get the best care possible."

Separated by blue painted doors, the kitchen and dining area were the only other rooms on the first floor. Two long wooden tables were surrounded by matching chairs and several highchairs where toddlers and young children could eat.

A wide-open staircase took us to the next level which was normally the living quarters of the Clark family. As we ascended the stairs, the sounds of crying grew even louder. An open hall at the top led to five bedrooms and a long veranda. Except for the master bedroom, babies were everywhere. Bright colored woven mats along with sheets on the tile floor provided flimsy protection where they lay closely together. The women workers were feeding, changing, holding, and comforting them. One woman was asleep on the mat with several children sleeping around her. Another quickly scooped up a sheet soaked with urine.

When we went back downstairs, Carol reminded me of the advice to rest a day after arrival to avoid succumbing to jet lag. We both agreed that we could not follow that warning with the pressing needs of the babies so obvious. I gestured to a worker that I wanted to feed a baby. She nodded and handed me the baby in her arms and pointed to the bottle on the table. I began to feed the baby and we smiled at one other, proud of our ability to communicate. Carol took my picture.

I watched with admiration as the women worked industriously. They had no doubt been taught to place sterile nipples onto sterilized bottles. On the same table as the clean bottles, however, a worker wiped pus from an infant's oozing boil, and laid another infant next to the drainage. Realizing they were not aware of the problems of cross-contamination, I pointed this out to Cherie. She explained to them in Vietnamese the problem of infection. The worker smiled and nodded repeatedly as Cherie spoke.

"I hope she doesn't resent my coming in here and correcting her work," I thought. But the woman continued with a smile making the necessary changes while giving the new instructions to her fellow workers.

"This one sure looks healthy," I commented as I went to another crying child. "Look at this big fat tummy," I cooed in baby talk.

"Sorry, LeAnn," Cherie explained gently, "but the protruding abdomen is probably a symptom of parasites."

The scale on the counter measured another baby's weight to be eight pounds. "That's a healthy newborn weight back home," Carol said, then looked at the infant's I.D. bracelet. With a nearly inaudible gasp she said, "This baby is three months old."

Some little bodies were infected with sores explained to be scabies. Naively, I asked why the infants weren't immunized or treated for these problems.

"It's all a matter of priorities and money," Cherie answered patiently. "We take those things for granted in the United States. Here, they're not even available much of the time. Keeping the children alive and fed is our first priority."

Oh, how I wanted one of these children ... or all of them ... forever.

Carol and I worked most of that day, going from baby to baby in a frantic attempt to help with feedings and diaper changings.

When our stomachs growled we commented privately about our hunger. But how could we speak out loud about that when starvation was obviously a very real problem here?

I stared at the noisy, needy babies laying all around me and remembered what Cherie had said in the car.

No, we weren't in the United States anymore.

This place was very different from Iowa.

As nighttime approached we visited in the office with Ross, Cherie, Sister Therese, and Thuy and discussed the upcoming airlift. Apparently the White House had been inundated with calls from adoption agencies and waiting adoptive families demanding that efforts be made to evacuate the orphans before the fall of Vietnam. That had prompted President Ford to instigate the airlift plan.

It was exciting to hear more about the children who left the night before. Because there was no clearance from Saigon or Washington, Cherie had called Cheryl Markson in Denver to get her opinion on participating in the flight. Cheryl knew every child at the Thu Duc Center and heartily agreed with efforts to evacuate them as soon as possible. All but three had been assigned families and each child had the required paperwork completed. Exit visas were the only thing lacking. That's what had annoyed the officials so.

Ross recalled the story, waving his arms and raising his voice for effect. "And as the plane was taking off, the control tower said 'you aren't cleared for takeoff' and ordered them to stop and return to the terminal. Tom Clark and Edward Daly just said, 'we can't hear you!' and just kept going and those kids were outta here!" he exclaimed, delighting in being part of such an adventure. "We got word they landed safely in Oakland, California though the U.S. government wasn't happy about them coming without Washington's okay. But hey! What are they going to do? How can you turn away a planeload of orphans, for gosh sakes!"

Ross was going to the Thu Duc Center then to pick up some needed supplies. He asked if Carol and I would like to accompany him, and we eagerly agreed. Because it was near sunset, we had to hurry to be back before curfew. It felt strange to be in a country where the government could tell you to be home by 10 o'clock.

The rickety Volkswagen van wound around the Saigon streets at dusk. The palm trees in the median swayed in the breeze. That picture of tranquility was interrupted when Carol nudged me and nodded toward a soldier whose head peered from the top of a sandbag fortress in the middle of the street.

This country was at war.

Traffic slowed, then came to an abrupt halt. An armed Vietnamese soldier approached the van.

"Ross, what's wrong? What is he going to do?" I asked in a low voice as Carol and I shared a nervous glance and fidgeted in our seats.

"Don't worry. It's routine," he answered, grinning at our troubled faces. After a brief verbal exchange, the soldier waved his gun in a gesture to move us forward. Ross explained that thousands of refugees from the Central Highlands were fleeing eastward to the coast as their provinces fell to the Communists. The police were afraid the flood of refugees would only complicate the defense of Saigon and bring Vietcong infiltrators into the city.

"Small Vietcong units have already sneaked into the suburbs," Ross said with a disturbing nonchalance. When he saw the horrified looks on our faces he quickly added, "Don't worry, Saigon won't fall for at least two or three months."

Somehow that didn't feel as comforting to me as he must have expected.

"April is the dry season," he said. "The summer rainy season always slows the fighting."

We were stopped by a second group of soldiers with hostile eyes. They also waved us on.

"There's a lot going on with President Thieu now," Ross continued. "As if the threat from the Vietcong wasn't enough for him to worry about, there's fear of a coup here. There's a group called the Action Committee for National Salvation that's trying to get him to resign, or at least give up his absolute power. They're even trying to reorganize the army to better defend Saigon and the Mekong Delta."

At the third and final roadblock we watched soldiers confronting some of the people crowded on the sidewalks. We looked at Ross for an explanation. In an effort to prevent riots or a possible coup attempt, a new law forbade civilians to congregate on the streets.

Thirty minutes later the van stopped close to the doorway of the wooden home that formerly housed the toddlers and children to age thirteen. The familiarity was comforting when I recognized it from the slide show I had presented dozens of times. The handmade jungle gym sat empty in the yard as a swing creaked slowly in the breeze. Inside, Carol and I looked around from room to room as Ross gathered supplies. The five remaining Vietnamese workers seemed to be at a loss as they gathered their things and prepared to return to the Center with us. They wore the same colorful smocks as those at the Giah Dinh Center but now they walked around aimlessly, picking up abandoned toys lying on the floors of the empty rooms. Sad thoughts vanished when Ross reminded us of the mission accomplished.

"It's hard to believe that the children who were crowded here only two days ago are now in the United States about to be placed in loving families. That's what we're all about!" His faced beamed with pride and his broad smile shone as he spoke.

He glanced at his watch. "Geez, it's getting late. We'd

better hurry. Or, if you'd rather, we can spend the night here. You've got to be exhausted." He extended both arms. "And there's plenty of room here!"

"It feels kind of scary," Carol said, knowing she spoke for both us.

"Afraid of cowboys?" Ross asked.

I could tell he was teasing, but I didn't understand.

He chuckled. "In Saigon, cowboys are young men who rob and loot places. They never physically hurt anyone, just steal."

I folded my arms and shivered slightly as I looked around the barren room. "I think we'd feel safer at the Center."

It was nearly dark as the van made its way back through empty streets. As he drove, Ross told of the beauty of Saigon and his love for the city and its people, a view not seen on the nightly news.

Cherie was shuffling papers on the desk when we arrived. "You'd both better get some sleep or you'll be no good. Jet lag usually hits the second day, and tomorrow we're going to keep you really busy."

She insisted that Carol and I take the master bedroom. She would sleep on the rattan couch in the office since Tom was gone. Reluctantly we agreed, no longer able to hide our fatigue.

The large master bedroom looked homey. How difficult it must have been to make a home for her own children in a city so upset with approaching war. The Clarks had four birth children and had adopted five others since living in Saigon. Among them were several teenage boys who would have been in the military service had it not been for the Clarks. Because so many male lives had been lost in a war spanning two generations, twelve-year-olds were often drafted for military service. There was talk that the local government had criticized the Clarks for their interference with this expectation and their boys kept a low profile to avoid problems.

The bedroom was filled with a dark, almost black wooden double bed with a tall square headboard, a dresser, and bunk beds where their youngest son, Brian, was already sleeping. He was a cheerful six-year-old with blond hair and pale-blue eyes.

We lay exhausted on the bed and whispered about the events of the day.

"Can you believe this?" seemed to be the hackneyed phrase as each event was retraced. We talked about what the following day might hold, but gradually gave ourselves over to the engulfing waves of sleep. The sheets smelled musty and clung to our damp skin. The humidity must have equaled the reported 96 degree temperature. As the ceiling fan continued its rotation we dozed.

BAM! BAM! BAM!

I bolted upright in bed, as did Carol beside me. Our heartbeats raced as our breathing stopped.

"What was that?" Carol gripped my arm. We heard a motorcycle drive away.

"Maybe just backfire from that motorbike." Six more blasts jolted us into each others arms.

"That's gunfire!"

"Oh, no!" I cried. "It is the war! The city IS being invaded!" By then Brian had run to our bed and buried his head in my lap, sobbing. Realizing that our fear would only heighten his, we both tried to be more calm to comfort him. "It'll be okay," I consoled as I rubbed his back gently. Angela and Christie loved that. For the first time since I had left them the thought ravaged my mind . . . I may never see my family again. I may die here. "I'm afraid the city *is* under attack," I whispered.

"Maybe the police have come for Cherie's sons. They said that could be a problem since they avoided the draft," Carol's voice quaked.

We crawled on our bellies to the veranda and cautiously peered over the railing, fearing our heads could be blown off as they rose above the ledge. The yard light of the Center lit up the street below and there was no sign of activity.

Crickets chirped.

We put the frightened child back in bed with unconvincing words of reassurance before we crept down the stairs.

Fear preceded and pursued us.

What if the soldiers are in the office?

What if they have Cherie?

Will we ever see our families again?

Should we just hide here upstairs?

That would be pretty cowardly, I decided, with our fellow workers being held captive downstairs.

We continued to tiptoe down the steps, gripping the handrail to support our trembling bodies.

The workers were asleep on the mats next to the children. How can they sleep when the place is under communist siege? Slowly we opened the door to the office to see Sister Therese typing. She turned to us in surprise.

"Why aren't you asleep?" she asked.

"We heard gunshots. We were terrified that the war was right here!" we answered.

"Cowboys," she said. "Probably stealing a few blocks away. The police sometimes fire shots to scare them. Or sometimes it's just the young boys who are soldiers. They often entertain themselves during the night by playfully shooting at rats, signs, or anything else handy."

We all laughed nervously at our overactive imaginations. We stayed to talk for a while, willing ourselves to calm down, then went back upstairs.

"No danger, honey," Carol said, kissing the little blond head. The boy smiled and rolled over to sleep. He seemed easily reassured.

No danger, Sister had said. Commonplace. Routine. I went out on the balcony and started to cry. My desire to complete our mission here was overpowered by my longing to go home. I went back to bed where Carol was tossing and turning.

"I can't go back to sleep," she groaned.

"I know," I whispered. "That always happens to me when gunshots wake me up." Our giggling eased the ache of fear. We sat cross-legged on the bed facing each other, held hands, and prayed together.

We prayed for our safety.

We prayed for our strength to accomplish whatever our purpose was on this mission.

We prayed for the faith to believe we'd be all right.

My weary body relaxed, but my mind did not. I was relieved when the dawn finally interrupted my worried thoughts. It's almost time to get on with the work . . . which takes us one step closer to home. Unexpectedly, that thought relaxed me enough that I finally succumbed to sleep.

Chapter Seven

I pulled my head from under the pillow and squinted as the sunshine glistened in the room. The silver lizard crawling on the ceiling reminded us that we were not at home. The day before I had tried to be nonchalant as I pointed out to Cherie that she had a lizard on her ceiling. She informed me it was a gecko, not a lizard, and said they were as common as house-flies in Iowa.

We rubbed sleep from our eyes and recalled the gunshot trauma in the night, trying to laugh at our naïveté as we dressed.

We opened the bedroom door and stepped into the hall and seemingly another world. "I've never heard 128 babies all wake up at the same time before," Carol mused as we hop-scotched over mats full of babies. We found a similar scene in the nursery where the workers greeted us with bright smiles and nods. "They're actually bathing and dressing every baby," I noticed with admiration and amazement.

We found Cherie working in the office . . . still. We related our nighttime war story to her, poking fun at ourselves.

And wondered if she ever slept.

Together we went to the kitchen. Cherie's teenage son, Ron, peddled up on his bicycle with fresh bread in the side basket. He combed his straight blond hair back with his fingers and joined us at the table. We had been warned not to drink anything but bottled beverages and to eat no fresh fruits or vegetables. Cherie agreed that we should follow that advice, so we washed down the warm bread with bottled cola.

The mood at the breakfast table was cheerful and fun as we recounted to Ross the hilarity of our actions the night before, each time dramatizing it a bit more.

It felt good to laugh.

It felt good to be there.

The meal seemed to feed my spirit as well as my body and I felt stronger again.

Cherie asked that we spend the day packing items needed for the transport of 200 babies to the United States. It was still very uncertain when our flight would be, but we needed to be ready. As we walked to the warehouse behind the Center, the cool air was tinged with a fresh fragrance and a new excitement. Cheerfully we entered the two-story building and looked around at the many rows of well-organized shelves and labeled boxes. We were witness to the five tons of supplies FCVN had shipped from the States every month.

Pulling a dusty box from a rack, Carol laughed. "How do we begin to find 600 sleepers and 1,000 Pampers?"

I pulled another labeled box from its place.

"Can you believe this! This box was sent from Iowa City! This is my handwriting! We packed this!" The significance of the work we'd been doing in Iowa City had never been so apparent. All the efforts, all the slide shows, all the speeches and time away from home had been worth it.

We sorted through the shirts, pants, and playsuits we recognized, delighting in the fact the clothes would return to the United States, this time on an infant.

For hours we worked separating clothes by size and gathering other items we thought would be useful for the trip.

"They're watching 'Sesame Street,' " I murmured.

"What?"

"Angela and Christie are watching 'Sesame Street' now. I

kept my watch on Iowa time so I can know what they're doing while I'm here. Angela is saying her numbers with the Count and Christie is scolding Oscar the Grouch."

Carol agreed that Chad would be watching the same program, but that Chris had outgrown that stage. For a brief moment a feeling of longing settled over us. Then with a deep breath, we returned to the important work at hand. The flight attendant had been right — we had a chance to change the lives of others.

It was much hotter inside the metal building. The heavy cardboard cartons, stacked four and five high, were covered with dust and mouse droppings. The air became ever more polluted with the feces and dirt brushed from the boxes. Periodically we went outside, coughing. That air was fresher, but it got muggier as the day grew longer. By noon, the lack of an adequate breakfast took its toll, and I admitted I was feeling faint.

"What we need is a sugar boost." I recalled the jellybeans I had confiscated before filling Angela's and Christie's Easter baskets. The truth was that I had bought and consumed four one-pound bags of jellybeans before the holiday and was often teased about my zealous appetite. Carol admitted that she too, was not feeling well, so I made my way to the Center and my flight bag to retrieve the candies. When I returned I found Carol with her head resting on a grimy box and looking quite pale.

"Here, these will help," I said as I handed her a fistful of assorted jellybeans.

With an ever so slight whine, Carol replied, "I only like orange ones."

I dropped to my knees and began laughing. "You're sitting here in a war-torn country in 105 degree heat, about to faint from lack of nourishment, and you only like orange ones?"

Carol started laughing so hard, she couldn't answer. She gasped for breath as she draped her body across the dirty boxes for support. I leaned back into a pile of sorted baby clothes and rolled from side to side, holding my stomach while we were lost in an extended period of howling.

Gradually we regained our composure and spent the next few hours completing that assignment. Still chuckling, we went to find Cherie in the office to see what we could do next. She had been at the embassy most of the day negotiating for the next flight out of Vietnam to the U.S. Thuy met us on the steps with great news.

"It looks like you'll be leaving with the babies today!" I cheered and clapped my hands, then hugged her and Carol.

"How soon do we leave?"

"*We* don't leave." Her smile disappeared. "You do. I'm not cleared to leave yet." Her voice dropped as she admitted, "I'm terrified to stay here. My government dislikes my involvement with an agency that takes children from our country. They accused me of buying and selling children. They do not understand that I only work to help them." She hung her head. "And I'm worried for my own children. I have an adopted five-year-old Vietnamese girl and a three-and-a-half-year-old Amerasian boy. What will become of them?" There was absolutely nothing I could do to help. I hugged her again.

Thirty minutes later Cherie returned to correct the rumor. "You're not leaving today. We didn't get it."

"What do you mean?" Carol and I asked in unison. Cherie dropped her folder of papers on the desk.

"Friends For All Children leaves today. The embassy staff doesn't know when we'll leave. Probably in the next few days."

I couldn't believe it.

It hadn't occurred to me that we wouldn't be the first agency allowed to leave. "Why not us?"

"They're punishing us for letting the Daly flight go without their approval. Our name's been taken from first place on the list."

"Isn't there anything we can do?" I asked, unable to conceal my disappointment. "You've worked so long and hard,

Cherie, you deserve the first flight out."

Recollections from the day before flashed in my mind. Memories of soldiers patrolling with weapons and the sounds of gunfire in the night. I knew that part of my protest was selfish. As committed as I was to this mission, I wanted to be on the first flight to leave.

My pleading was to no avail. Cherie said her hands were tied and that FFAC would have that privilege.

"See, Mr. Daly had originally arranged for FFAC to fly 450 orphans out last night. But then AID told them his DC-8 might not be safe."

"Who's AID?" I interrupted, trying to get this story straight.

"The Agency for International Development. They're working on the airlift. But when FFAC heard the flight might not be safe, they declined his offer. That's when he called us. Ed Daly has such a devotion and love of these orphans, I trusted his judgment and arrangements completely. That's when we got the kids at the Thu Duc Center ready and out in one hour. It was only after his gutsy . . . and I might mention . . . safe, flight that AID announced its plans to take 2,000 orphans out."

Cherie must have seen the discouraged look still on our faces.

"It's only right that Friends For All Children gets this flight," Cherie said. She pointed out that Rosemary Taylor's kids would be on board. She had committed the last five years of her life to orphan relief in South Vietnam.

"There are several church groups and seven private adoption agencies in Vietnam, and everybody wants to be first." She sighed. "FCVN was the first agency to be licensed in Vietnam. I just hope we're not the last to leave."

We tried to mask our disappointment and envy as it was obvious Cherie felt bad enough already.

"That's okay," I said lightly.

"That'll just give us more time to get ready for our flight, which will surely be next," Carol added. She was so confident now and didn't seem to feel the same urgency as I. We all smiled weakly at each other and muttered words of agreement.

Cherie didn't seem to hear as her eyes fixed on an old car making its way slowly into the driveway. "Mai," was all she said.

"I can't believe she's here," Thuy whispered looking over Cherie's shoulder.

Cherie's face glowed as she told us about the child FCVN's president Cheryl Markson and her husband Mick had been trying to adopt for seven years. In 1969 Mick had been stationed for a year in the Central Highlands near the Domanie de Marie orphanage by Dalat. Like many American G.I.s he had devoted time, energy, and love to help the orphans.

"That's when he fell in love with Mai. She was three then and they've been working to adopt her ever since," Cherie said as she watched the dilapidated car approach the house. "Cheryl and Mick have visited her several times over the years—as recently as two months ago. The nuns have told me stories of how the Vietcong sometimes came to the all-girls orphanage and took it over as a command post. To protect the girls, the nuns would sometimes hide them. Mai spent two days under a mattress once."

Two nuns stepped out of the car. Then exited a beautiful Asian girl in a white blouse and blue jumper, her school uniform, followed by a seven-year-old in a white straw hat. The older girl tried to hide her pudgy, round face behind the nuns in their long, flowing, black habits. Cherie slowly approached the child, and squatted to her level. We watched as Cherie spoke quietly to her. Mai shook her head back and forth as Cherie continued to talk. A few minutes later Cherie came up the steps, her eyes red.

"She's afraid to come. The nuns have raised her since she was a baby. They're all she knows. They're her family. Yet when Mick was here last year one of the nuns asked Mai, 'Do you want to go live with Mr. Markson?' and she answered in Vietnamese, 'Yes, he's my daddy.' "

The nuns bent down to hug and whisper to the child.

Cherie continued, "The young nun is Sister Katrina. She has been Mai's housemother — her mother for that matter — most of her life. She would do anything for that child. A few weeks ago the Vietcong invaded Dalat and the nuns had to evacuate the orphanage. They put all the girls into the back of an old beat-up truck and headed for the coast. Masses of people and orphans were there hoping to find a way out of the country. Sister Katrina wanted to try one last time to get Mai to us . . . to the Marksons. She helped make a raft and about a dozen people spent three days on it in the South China Sea and floated to the inlet by Saigon. She put Mai in a cardboard box to keep her from falling overboard. When she got into Saigon she didn't have our address or phone number so she went to the St. Vincent de Paul polio center for orphans. She knew the Sisters of Charity would let them stay there a few days. She said she just trusted God would help her find us. And help He did. Two days ago Thuy and I went there to see if they had orphans relinquished for the airlift. Thuy looked out the window, and there standing next to the pool that the G.I.s built, stood Mai. It was like a miracle! The Sisters of Charity didn't know the whole story and wouldn't let her go then. They said they'd bring her to us later. But we didn't know until this moment whether the Markson's dream would come true."

The nuns stood, took Mai by the hand and moved toward the house.

"They know she has no future here," Cherie went on. "With the country expected to fall soon, they have no choice now but to let her go, for her own welfare."

Mai began to cry. Tears dripped from one nun's cheeks as she bent to give her one last hug. Cherie walked back to Mai, took her hand, and slowly led her to the steps as the nuns got

71

back into their battered van and drove away. The tearful child waved good-bye to the only family she had ever known.

Our attention turned to the little girl wearing a white straw hat with part of the brim folded back. She stood absolutely expressionless and silent. They said the child's mother had carried her from Da Nang to Saigon.

Cherie told her story. "The mother told the nuns that this little girl witnessed the slaughter of half-white children in Da Nang. Because she is Amerasian, the mother feared for her life. She pulled the wide-brimmed hat down over her little girl's face and carried her over 300 miles to the orphanage for protection."

We listened in silence, sobered by the horror we could hardly believe.

"No wonder she sits with such a blank look on her face," said Carol. "She's seen a bit of hell."

Twenty-one children from the Center were scheduled on a flight to Australia that afternoon. Carol and I returned to the warehouse where we collected supplies for the trip. I had been unaware that FCVN placed children in other countries and was impressed with the international scope of the organization.

In scorching heat we began to load babies into the Volkswagen van. The middle seat had been removed and I sat on the back bench seat as Ross handed me baby after baby. The first ones were settled on the seat next to me. Then we began placing them side by side on the mats laid on the floorboards. As they were packed in, kicking and waving their hands, one baby after another began to cry. The cries of twenty-one unhappy, uncomfortable infants echoing inside the hollow, metal van created a deafening symphony.

As nurses and moms we were used to crying babies, but this was unlike anything we had ever imagined. There was very little we could do. As the doors were shut and the air inside the van grew hotter, the little ones became more upset.

Carol climbed into the front passenger seat and picked up two babies to cradle in her arms, hoping to quiet them. Ross started the van and we crept into the narrow street with our precious, cacophonous cargo. Another vehicle followed behind carrying supplies and Tuong, one of Ross' shadows. He was an adoring eleven-year-old orphan with a crippled leg.

"He got kicked off the World Airways flight last night," Ross said. "No boys over ten-years-old are allowed to leave the country. Guess they want to make a soldier out of him too in the next year or so." The young boy would help us load babies and supplies onto the waiting plane. As we moved slowly through Saigon toward the airport, Ross kept glancing back at the cargo of bedlam to assure himself that everything was still okay. Carol and I steadied the children on the floor with our feet, trying to keep them from rolling against one another, while occasionally shouting over the din to each other. If they hadn't been packed in so closely, there might have been problems, but there was nowhere for these babies to roll.

"Don't worry, little ones," Carol whispered to the babies she cuddled in her arms. "Soon you'll be safe and free."

"We've got to stop at the Australian Embassy first," Ross hollered. The hum of the van's engine seemed to calm the fussing infants and the breeze through the opened windows abated the hundred-degree heat. He parked the van at the curb and nudged his way through a crowd of dozens to get inside. During the hour-long wait the babies began to perspire and cry. We held them two and three at a time hoping to pacify them so we could save the formula for their plane trip. We opened the van door but the muggy outside air did little to help.

A man leaving the embassy came to the van and introduced himself as Doug Gray. I'd heard much about his home for blind and crippled orphans in Saigon and felt honored to meet him. He explained that he had come to the embassy to plead that his ten-year-old polio victims be allowed to leave.

The Vietnamese government denied his request.

"No ten-year-old males can leave Vietnam," he quipped, imitating the stubborn officials. I had heard rumors about handicapped orphans being murdered by the Vietcong and was afraid the rumors might be based on a kernel of truth. As I suppressed my own anger, I wondered how Doug and others like him could live with the frustration on a daily basis.

"It's bloody chaos in there!" He nodded toward the building. "There is a rumor that Australia is granting unlimited visas to South Vietnamese," he added, explaining the crowd. "I hear the French Embassy is being overrun with people too. When the French left in 1954, they permitted over 50,000 Vietnamese to settle there. Panicking people are hoping they will do the same now."

Finally Ross came scurrying from the building with the necessary paperwork and hopped into the driver's seat. It was a twenty-minute drive to the airport. It seemed our goal was finally in sight.

But as we reached the airport drive, traffic stopped abruptly. In front of us, near the end of the runway, an enormous black cloud billowed into the sky.

"Oh, no! What's that, Ross?"

"Probably just some sort of test. Remember, this is a military base, not just an airport. You see this kind of thing all the time." I stifled my doubt and forced myself to believe his explanation.

Ross drove to an entrance gate. When we identified ourselves, one soldier motioned us through.

"You can come in," he said, "but your plane has been delayed."

Delayed? We looked at each other. Delay is a nuisance on a pleasure trip. But for a vanload of infants in this heat? We knew dehydration was our biggest worry.

"I'd better find the van carrying the supplies and formula," said Ross. He immediately climbed out and loped off across the tarmac.

Chapter Seven

For the next hour Carol and I frantically tried to comfort the babies. Despite our best efforts, the blankets beneath each of them them became wet with sweat and tears. We knew they could ill afford the loss of precious body fluids, so we held one in each arm and rocked several on our laps at the same time.

But the others kept crying.

A man approached the van and identified himself as an Australian reporter. He wore a brown safari hat and khaki clothing and spoke in a delightful brogue. Glad for any distraction, we asked if he knew anything about the babylift to his country that these little ones waited for in desperation.

"Why, yes ma'am," he said, his face clouding. "The flight is delayed while airline employees search the plane for bombs."

"*Bombs?*" I asked, incredulous yet again.

"You mean . . . you haven't heard?" he asked, and he took a deep breath. "The first planeload of orphans enroute to the United States crashed just after takeoff. They suspect sabotage."

"No! That can't be true." I said. Panic fluttered inside me.

"It's absolutely true," he insisted. "Didn't you see the fire trucks and the black cloud from the explosion?"

"Yes, I saw them."

"Well, that's why. There was either a bomb on board that plane or it was shot down."

Carol looked at me as if she didn't know what to believe. Dumbfounded, I grew angry with the Australian messenger. This was exactly how rumors got started in the first place. "Ross said they're just testing. I don't believe you. Who would bomb babies?"

"Well, the government has not been excited or cooperative about this babylift plan. Maybe they're sending a message."

I kept arguing. If I believed this could happen, then all the goodness I had seen since I had been in Saigon would seem false. It simply wasn't possible. No one, not even here in this place so damaged by war, could deliberately bomb a plane full of babies. Could they?

Shortly after the reporter left, Ross returned to the van. He had heard the same report and said he didn't know whether to believe it either. But he thought it was possible.

I still refused to believe it could happen but since the plane to Australia was ready to load, we ended our debate. With a baby in each arm, I entered the aircraft and halted, immobilized by the sight. Hundreds of crying babies covered the floor of the plane. Canvases were stretched across parallel bars about six inches off the floor with twelve-inch aisles between them. Babies lay shoulder to shoulder on the long hammock-like rigs with a long seat belt extended across their bodies for the entire length of the plane.

"LeAnn." Ross' voice broke my trance and he handed me two more babies. I in turn handed them to an Australian volunteer on board. Three men identified themselves as Australian members of Parliament who were facilitating the evacuation.

"It must be 100 degrees in there," I warned as I stepped off the plane for more babies.

"Once it gets in the air it will be properly cooled." A nearby Australian explained the makeshift arrangements. "We'll ride this way only to Bangkok where proper arrangements can be made. For the sake of these babies' lives, we need to get as many out as fast as we can. Any baby we leave behind is at risk." He gestured toward the plane. "These 300 will be saved!"

"Of course you're right," I said quickly. "If we waited for ideal accommodations it would be too late."

Carol, Ross, eleven-year-old Tuong, and I carried the final few infants to the plane's ramp.

"No more room," came a shout from inside.

"But we have six more!"

"We'll make do," the brogue reassured us. "Bring them in. We'll make room for them in this cardboard box and secure it in here." My heart was torn as I relinquished the baby in my arms.

"They deserve better," I grumbled, swallowing back tears.

"In seven hours they'll be in Australia where they'll live happily ever after," the Parliament member said with a wink.

The supplies were finally loaded and Ross held the last of the infants out to Tuong, the young boy who had been helping us. Looking into the eyes of the orphan who idolized him, Ross spoke quietly so nearby soldiers couldn't hear.

"When you carry this last baby onto the plane, stay there."

Tuong stared incredulously at Ross. Slowly the look of bewilderment on his thin face turned to one of fear as he realized what he was being told to do.

Fighting tears, Ross tried to explain. "You have no future here, my friend. Even with your bad leg, you'll be drafted into the army. In Australia you'll be free, safe, and healthy. Now go."

The boy stood staring silently into the face of this man who'd given him love when no one else would.

"Go," Ross repeated.

The boy limped forward and threw his arms around Ross. They were both crying now.

Ross patted him on the back. "Believe you'll make it and you will."

With one final look into Ross' eyes, the boy turned, took the infant, and carried it onto the plane. He took a seat across from the doorway and sat nervously, his eyes pinned on Ross. Ross kept smiling and gave him a thumbs up as a Vietnamese soldier patrolled the aisle, checking the passengers.

Ross' smile never wavered despite his fear that the youngster would be discovered. "If they find this stowaway our future flights out of here could be in trouble," he muttered to us, still smiling. Carol and I looked on as the soldier made one last trip down the aisle, then stepped off and motioned for the door to be shut. As the door closed, Ross nodded and winked to reassure his small, frightened friend.

The plane slowly taxied away, carrying one extra child who would never have escaped otherwise. As it disappeared down the runway, Ross could contain his excitement no longer.

"He made it! He made it!" He danced gleefully around and then grabbed Carol and me in a bear hug.

We started across the tarmac to the van, but our happiness was quickly dimmed as our eyes were once again drawn to the cloud of smoke still at the end of the runway.

"It can't be true, can it, Ross?" Carol asked again, obviously hoping for reassurance.

"I don't know," he answered grimly. "Let's get back to the Center. Cherie will know."

Ever since the gunshots scared us in the night, my confidence had been faltering. I could feel the remains of it shatter while we walked across the pavement toward the van. When we passed a gigantic Pan Am jetliner, I fought back a compulsion to run to it and climb on board and fly home to Mark. To my girls.

It suddenly seemed that good-byes in Vietnam were too often too sudden.

And final.

Chapter Eight

As we drove away from the airport, I looked over my shoulder at the plumes of black smoke. The sound of rescue helicopters battered the air overhead. I barely noticed the crowds
and the noise around us on the streets of Saigon as we returned to the orphanage. Could the Australian be right? Had
babies and escorts really been killed on a flight sabotaged
before leaving Vietnam? We talked quietly, trying to convince ourselves that it wasn't true.

It couldn't be.

Ross slowly drove the van through the gates of the orphanage. We would tell Cherie the rumor. She would know.

But inside, the office was already awash with grief.

Cherie threw her arms around Ross as we entered and
through her tears confirmed that the worst was true. The
Friends For All Children flight had crashed. Many of the
babies and escorts had been killed.

Both Cherie and Sister Therese had friends who died in the
crash. Sister sobbed into her handkerchief as she told us
about a young friend who had been on the plane, Sister
Christina, and all the good she had done.

"The news reports are saying it was our babies who
crashed," Cherie cried on Ross' shoulder. "I drove like mad
to the airport and they told me it wasn't us, but FFAC. Dear

God, how could this happen?"

Overcome by the grief and panic all around me, I sank down on a rattan couch and sobbed uncontrollably. The flight I fought to be on had crashed. If I had gotten my way, we would likely be dead. What in the world had made me believe I was invulnerable?

Carol had almost convinced herself not to come. Now I wished she had succeeded in convincing us both to stay home. In Iowa. Where the war was so distant.

That brought my thoughts back to my family. I imagined the girls playing happily at Diane's home and I could almost hear Mark strumming his guitar and singing softly in our living room. They were probably sound asleep right then, the Iowa sun just peeking over the cornfields.

Carol, the Carol who had nearly backed out of coming to Vietnam, led me out the door and onto the steps. where I stood hugging myself, wanting to go home.

The rescue helicopters continued to beat their terrible rhythm overhead and ambulance sirens screamed.

"We've got to get out of here," I pleaded. "If they bombed one flight, they'll bomb the next one too. What have I done to my family? Will I ever see them again?" I could hardly get my breath as sobs wracked my body.

Carol cradled me in her arms. "Sure you will," she said soothingly. "Even if it was a bomb, they'll never let that happen again. And we don't even know if it was a bomb or if it was even deliberate. We'll be fine. I know we will."

We'll be fine. That's what I'd told her all the way to Vietnam. Could she have been as afraid then as I was now? And if she was, how had she ever found the courage to board the plane in San Francisco? It must have taken every ounce of strength she had. I had bulled through it—but my faith and courage crashed into the rice paddies with that plane.

"We *will* be okay," Carol consoled. "I have complete faith that next week at this time we'll be watching 'Sesame Street' with the kids."

Chapter Eight

"I know Mark didn't want me to come in the first place. And now I know he was right. He'll be getting up pretty soon. He always listens to the news on the radio while he shaves in the mornings. He'll hear about the plane crash. How will he know I wasn't on it? I can't stand to think of the pain I'm causing."

"Let's go inside and see about calling home," Carol said, giving me a gentle pat on the back. I mopped the tears from my puffy eyes and nodded, forcing a smile.

Inside the office, things seemed calmer. My heart sank again, though, when we learned there were no phone lines available out of Saigon. How naive I had been to think I could just pick up the phone and dial home.

The room was congested with people who came to offer support or exchange information.

"The C-5A skidded over one rice paddy, then a river, then crashed into a second paddyfield."

"Both wings snapped off, a fire started, and finally the plane, six stories high, broke into four pieces."

"Nearly 250 orphans were on board."

"Half of them died."

"Fifteen to twenty adults were pulled out alive."

"The rest are either dead, injured, or trapped in the wreckage."

"Baby bottles, pacifiers, and comic books were strewn around the crash site."

An American husband and wife, who were Wycliffe Bible translators, were among those who came to offer help. He was a paunchy, middle-aged balding man in a sweat-stained white shirt. His wife was dressed in a small patterned plain dress and had long, light-brown hair braided and rolled around her head. They suggested we kneel on the floor and bow our heads as the husband prayed for those killed, the survivors, and for peace. Carol joined them and prayed as she knelt. My mind was a hurricane of emotions. I knelt feeling numb, hardly aware of their prayer.

Ross whispered something to Cherie, then held her as she cried again. "Dolly and some of her kids died in the crash," he said to Sister who joined in the embrace. He looked at us and explained how she had been married to a Vietnamese man and gave many of her gifts to help the orphans while she lived there.

Carol and I went upstairs on the veranda and sat in the quiet night, trying to swallow some of the rice supper the Vietnamese cook had prepared. Sorrow blanketed the air. Cherie came upstairs and quietly joined us.

"Cherie," my voice quivered. "I'm sorry to have to say this, but I can't stay here and finish this airlift. I need to go home." I felt like a quitter and a coward. I must have presented a pitiful sight to this woman who had lost her own friends today, but she just looked at me and smiled.

Finally she spoke. "I know how you must feel, LeAnn, but there is no way out of Saigon now. No boat, no plane is allowed to leave. This isn't Iowa, you know," she teased. "You can't just go buy a ticket and leave whenever you want. Here in Vietnam the government says when and how you leave. The best and maybe the only way out of here is on the babylift."

I sat silently for a moment, looking at Cherie's and Carol's reassuring faces.

I managed a lopsided smile. "Guess I've decided to stay," I said with a little laugh.

* * *

In Iowa

The ringing of the phone seemed to be a part of the bad dream he was having. By the fifth or sixth ring Mark stumbled to the kitchen and took the receiver from the wall phone. His usual early morning stupor was compounded by exhaustion. His fitful night's sleep had been interrupted by vomiting and diarrhea.

Chapter Eight

"Hello," he said in a confused, groggy voice. The caller identified himself as a reporter from the local newspaper.

"Was your wife on the plane that crashed in Saigon last night?"

Suddenly Mark was alert, fear throbbing inside him. "What are you talking about?"

Immediately the reporter apologized. "I thought surely you had heard the news by now. A planeload of orphans and escorts crashed after takeoff in Saigon last night."

Mark squinted to see the clock on the wall reading 7 A.M. Still apologizing, the reporter promised to use his connections with the Associated Press to learn if Carol and I had been passengers on that fateful flight.

Mark's mind raced with panic, confusion, and grief as he fumbled to make coffee.

"Why didn't he call AP first?" he grumbled angrily, "Instead of asking me!"

His hands trembled as he scooped coffee into the pot. "How long will it be till I know if my wife is alive?"

* * *

Diane turned down the volume on the TV set in the kitchen as she called the kids to the breakfast table. She blotted her eyes with a dishtowel then pretended to be cheerful as she served pancakes to the happy foursome. Mom had called her earlier. No, she hadn't heard anything either. Only the horrible reports and pictures of the crash on the morning news.

As she washed syrup from Angela's and Christie's fingers, she hugged them long and hard before they skipped off to play.

* * *

"Eight!" Chris said to his Dad. "Hey Chad! There have

been eight calls about Mom!"

Chris loved numbers, so keeping track of the many phone calls was kind of a game for him. Al hadn't told the boys about the frantic call from Carol's father earlier that morning waking him out of a sound sleep.

"Did you hear about the plane crash?" he asked Al. "The first plane of orphans out of Saigon crashed!"

He had called Mark. They both felt numb. No one knew anything. He watched Chad play happily on the floor. So many questions were unanswered.

"Could I have talked her out of this? Why didn't I try harder?"

* * *

In Denver

Cheryl bolted out of bed for the 3 A.M. phone call. When he heard his wife crying, Mick was at her side.

"That was Leah, from the Georgia chapter." She took a deep breath to steady her voice. "A ham radio operator there heard that a planeload of orphans crashed in Vietnam."

They held each other and cried together for an hour, wondering how such a catastrophe could happen and how they would cope if it had. Then they attempted to call Cherie in Saigon.

"We cannot place a call to Saigon at this time," the operator said. "However, we'll be happy to book you a phone call in July."

"July! July! There may not be a South Vietnam in July!" Cheryl slammed the receiver.

At 5 A.M. they called the State Department.

"Bernie Salvo, please," she requested, pacing the path in the carpet. She had been talking to Bernie every day the past week to get an update on the situations near Saigon and Dalat, where they thought their future daughter Mai was. Bernie had served in Vietnam with Mick. If anyone would tell them the truth now it would be Bernie.

"Vietnam desk, Bernie Salvo."

Cheryl told him what she had heard. "Tell me it's not true," she begged.

"There's information coming in on the crash, Cheryl, but we haven't been able to confirm who was in it. That's why I haven't called you."

She knew about the board where all travel in and out of Vietnam was posted. She dared to ask, "Who was on the board as the next expected flight out, Bernie?"

"FCVN."

"Oh, no!"

"We don't know for sure, Cheryl. Let me keep on this. I'll call you as soon as I know anything." The soothing tone to his voice could not abate the panic swelling inside her.

With robot-like motion, she dressed for work. Cherie Clark had sent her three preschoolers to stay with Cheryl the week before since the work in Saigon consumed her time. "Don't tell Johanna, Tahn, or Jeni what's going on yet," she said to Mick who was dressing to go with her. "Oh, no, Mick! What if their mom was on that flight? Or Ross? Or LeAnn and Carol?"

"Stop," he coaxed, hugging her again. "Let's go to the office and wait for the call."

Ever since the news of the Daly flight, FCVN had been inundated with phone calls and letters. The mailman had toted a shoulder pack for years, but now arrived in a truck to deliver the mountains of mail. Hundreds of caring people sent money and others requested adoption information. Many whose dossiers were already on file called to inquire about the status of their future son or daughter.

Cheryl forced herself to continue preparations to go from her home in Denver to Oakland where the Daly flight had landed. Thoughts of the plane crash exploded in her mind. The office phone rang nonstop. When they couldn't get a line for outgoing calls, they decided to go back home to continue business. Reporters from Associated Press and local stations greeted them, then stood watch on their lawn for much of the day.

Cheryl answered the phone with the receiver wedged between her shoulder and her ear while shuffling papers in her hands. "Hello?"

"I'm glad the little _____ are dead, and I hope the rest die too," said the woman in a monotone.

"Who is this?" Cheryl could hardly comprehend what she was hearing.

"You deserve this. Your own kids deserve what happened to them."

Cheryl dropped the phone. Screams erupted from her mouth. No words. Just a continuous shrill of horror. Mick held her tight until the hysterical screaming turned to sobs.

"We've lost everything," she cried. "It's all over." When his efforts to calm her were futile, Mick called the doctor. The prescribed sedation allowed her to sleep. She had not allowed herself that luxury during the chaotic days past.

Another 3 A.M. phone call jolted her from bed. She raced down the hall bumping into walls, through the dining room to the kitchen. She yanked the phone to her ear.

"Cheryl, this is Cherie." At first her voice was clear, then it began to fade. "It wasn't us!"

"What?" Cheryl wanted to hear this message right.

"It wasn't us!" Cherie shouted again.

The tidal wave of joy she felt receded when she heard. "It was FFAC. It was supposed to be us, but US-AID canceled us because they were so mad about the Daly flight going without their okay." Then through tears Cherie added, "Margaret's dead."

Cheryl's eyes burned. Margaret Moses, from Australia, was the spirit and drive of Friends For All Children.

"She traded places with Wendy. Call FFAC and tell them Wendy is alive. So are about half the kids."

Chapter Eight

The signal was getting much weaker. She thought she heard Cherie giggling.

"We've got Mai!"

"What?"

"We've got Mai!" Cherie yelled again with a fading laugh.

"You've got Mai?" Mick jumped to her side. "It's not our plane!" she told him. "She's got Mai!" The line went dead. She dropped the phone and twirled in her husband's arms as they cried and took turns repeating, "They've got our Mai!"

Cheryl laughed for the first time in days. She had been momentarily lifted from the bowels of hell to the top of the world. Although grieving would return for those who were lost, she allowed herself joy for those feared dead, but now known alive. "Thank You, God."

Chapter Nine

The tragedy only intensified the fever pitch of our airlift plans. In the office, Cherie reviewed with us the work to be done that evening. As I listened to my assignment, I tried to fake a positiveness that still evaded me. The phone rang.

"LeAnn, it's for you," Sister said.

I almost laughed. It seemed like a joke. "Who'd call me in Saigon?"

An Associated Press reporter was on the line. An Iowa City reporter had contacted a chain of reporters across the Pacific in which he was the final link, to learn if I had been on the fatal crash. The reporter assured me the same chain would begin in reverse until ultimately the Iowa City reporter would call Mark and inform him of our safety. The man asked if I had any other messages for my husband.

Any messages. There was so much I wanted to say. So much he needed to know.

"Just tell him I'm okay and I love him very much."

As I hung up the phone, tears swelled in my eyes.

"Oh, thank You, God!" I slumped onto the couch next to Carol. "My family will know I'm alive and well! Their not knowing was killing me inside." The relief was immediate, bringing with it a surge of energy and enthusiasm. "So let's get to work!"

News of the crash did not slow the arrival of more children, of all ages, to the Center. The building became even more crowded wall to wall with little ones and workers. Many foster mothers and several Vietnamese nurses came to help. Blankets covered every inch of floor space and babies covered every inch of the blankets. A baby boy in blue pajamas sat quietly in an infant seat. He was severely deformed with a cleft lip and palate. One worker sat patiently feeding him. The walls and floors vibrated with the sounds of crying and chattering.

I was drawn to help the workers with the bedlam of babies as that noisy need was so obvious. But that was only a part of the work to be done before the airlift.

The Saigon government had issued many requirements for the exportation of the children. We had a lot of paperwork to do in very limited time. Each child needed a legal name and a birth certificate. The irony was the government had denied birth certificates to newborns previously because it was too much paperwork when many of them died anyway, Cherie explained. Only after babies were a few months old were birth certificates routinely issued.

Included in the eighteen boxes of supplies we brought were hospital ID bracelets. We began the bizarre task of assigning Vietnamese names to each infant. Many had been given names or nicknames by the staff, but few had legal names. Cherie explained there were many birthing centers throughout the city and country. The destitute young women would come to deliver their children, then leave them to be cared for by others since they were certain they would not be able to provide for them. These kids were said to be abandoned at birth. What a sad phrase.

"What an immeasurable amount of love it must have taken for a mother to give up her baby," I said half out loud. It was almost inconceivable to me.

"If she was an unwed mother or if the baby was not full Vietnamese, she really didn't have the option to keep it,"

Cherie explained. "It just isn't done here. It's impossible. This is a very family-oriented, patriarchal society. You are who your father is. That's why the half-Caucasian kids have such a problem. The families cannot accept them. It's no wonder, then, why so many Amerasian girls turn to prostitution to get by."

She must have seen me squinting and shaking my head as I tried to grasp what she was saying.

She went on. "Here the Vietnamese don't adopt kids unless they are family members. You must know the family lines. By the same token, if an orphan has relatives they're usually not adoptable. The extended family is expected to take care of their own."

One of the volunteer physicians, Dr. Cuong, was there to assess each baby and estimate its age if birth information was not available. As he provided the information, we provided a name to print on each ID bracelet. Sister Therese and Phoung, the Vietnamese secretary, typed the names in distinctive green ink. "So our kids can't be easily mixed up with others," Cherie had said. I couldn't imagine what she meant or how that could happen.

"Hey, this is Jeni," Ross said of a cute baby in his arms. "That's all we've ever called her."

"Jeni ain't gonna cut it getting her out of the country," Sister Therese teased as she looked in her book of Vietnamese names.

"Is this legal?" Carol couldn't help but ask.

"We didn't make up the rules to this game, they did," Cherie replied. "We just have to find a way to comply."

"It seems like the government is deliberately making regulations impossible to meet in such a short period of time," Carol said as she attached bracelets to the ankle and wrist of the infant squirming in her arms.

"Some say that's because immigration is still mad about the Daly flight," Ross said with a smirk.

"You have to remember, the Vietnamese are a very proud

people. Its hard for them to admit that they can't take care of their own." Cherie offered. She had so much to teach us about Vietnam and its people, but it was evident our only conversations would be as she worked. "They have a strong cultural identity and don't accept the common . . . and sometimes chauvinistic . . . American view that their orphans can do no better than to come to the U.S. Ideally, I wish they could live here happily ever after, but that doesn't look even remotely possible."

"I read there are 1.5 million orphans in Vietnam," Ross added, raising his pitch to be heard above the complaining babies. "The great majority of them are cared for by relatives or neighbors. Like Cherie said, they are proud to take care of their own. But 40,000 of them are outcasts because they are racially mixed . . . offsprings of our long-departed American G.I.s. These are the kids in big trouble. Especially the half black ones." He nodded to the dark-skinned baby in his arms and gave her a little hug.

Sister Therese continued to feverishly page through her book and chuckles turned to laughter as Ross began concocting silly, rhyming names for the babies. It felt good to laugh again.

As we worked, Carol stopped suddenly and looked at me.

"I just thought of someone else who likely heard about the crash and may think we were on it."

"Who?"

"The flight attendant." She frowned. "I wish he could somehow know we were safe. It would be awful if he spends the rest of his life thinking he talked me into going on a mission that ended my life." Hopefully through his airline he could find out the truth. If he had in fact been a guardian angel, he would already know.

A little girl appeared at Carol's side. She looked to be about six years old with sad, dark eyes and straight black hair cropped short so her little ears showed through. She wore a short pink dress and stood shyly next to Carol with a little pink purse draped over her arm. Carol spoke to her softly and the child spoke back in Vietnamese. Carol beamed and winked at me. The petite princess didn't smile easily but was obviously drawn to Carol. While we worked through much of the night, the little girl stayed close at her side.

Eventually the child's eyes revealed her fatigue. Carol took her to the rattan couch and motioned for her to lie down and sleep. She then kissed her cheek and returned to the desk to work. But when she turned around, the girl was at her elbow again. When Carol smiled down at her the little one smiled back. Carol suggested that they both get ready for bed and sleep as she figured it would be the only way the girl would rest. The child seemed to understand and opened her purse. Her whole face smiled as she proudly produced a toothbrush.

As they lay together on the couch, the little girl snuggled closer to Carol, her purse clenched tightly in her hands. I knew Carol's motherly instincts were in full swing as she missed her sons so far away. She lay watching the brown ceiling fan turn and was lulled to sleep.

Two hours later she woke, the little girl still cuddled close to her. The room was dark and unusually quiet. She seemed surprised to see me sitting at the desk writing.

"What are you doing?"

"I'm writing. If I don't write all this down right away, I'm afraid I'll forget."

"I don't think we'll ever forget today," Carol murmured and went back to sleep. I rolled my coat up as a pillow and lay on the rug of the office floor. I watched the gecko statue-like on the wall.

No, I didn't think I'd ever forget today either.

Chapter Ten

I opened my eyes slowly, expecting to see the framed picture of Madonna and Child hanging on the wall next to my bed at home. I blinked repeatedly as I focused instead on the brown gecko still clinging to the ceiling.

"Oh, good. You're awake," Carol said in a hushed tone. "LeAnn, you'll never believe what I just saw." The sadness in her voice told me I probably wouldn't want to believe it either. She sat on the floor next to me, her new little friend huddled at her side.

"When I woke up, I went to the nursery to see what Cherie was up to at this hour. She and the doctor were working over one of the cribs. I could see the sleeves of his white lab coat rolled up to his elbows and the sweat on his forehead. He was trying to resuscitate a baby. Then he looked up at Cherie and shook his head. LeAnn, I watched a baby die!" Her voice caught. "The other workers in the room had stopped to watch. They looked so sad, then turned and went back to work. Cherie looked like she was about to cry as she slowly covered the tiny body with a sheet." Her eyes brimmed with tears and her little friend nestled closer as if to comfort her. "To think this probably happens every day here. It breaks my heart." With our arms around each other, we sat in silence.

Back in the States our world had clipped along, functioning in what we believed was a normal fashion. But here, life was fragile and easily snuffed out.

When Cherie and Ross joined us in the kitchen for breakfast, they smiled to see Carol's little friend huddled next to her at the table. Carol gently wiped food from around the girl's mouth and gazed adoringly into her eyes. I had seen her give that same look of motherly love to her sons many times before. She and Al had no plans to adopt, but I knew she was serious when she teased about the possibility of this little girl fitting into their family.

"So what are the plans for my little shadow?" she asked casually. Cherie said the youngster would be going to live with her grandmother in California. I could see the flicker of hope she felt as she had cuddled the child in the night was extinguished.

Carol responded quickly, "I'm happy she has a family to love her."

"Speaking of which," Cherie began, breaking a piece of soft bread from the loaf. "LeAnn, you and Mark will be adopting one of those babies in the next room. You can wait to be assigned one from across a desk in Denver," she paused to touch my hand, "or you can go in there and choose a son."

I was stunned speechless.

I felt myself flush with excitement—then with fear.

"Really?" I finally croaked. Surely I had heard her wrong. Cherie's tired eyes danced. "Really."

"So I can just go in there and pick out a son?"

Carol and Ross chuckled at my inability to comprehend her message. Cherie nodded again.

I turned to Carol. "Come with me." She jumped up immediately and we approached the door to the nursery together.

I paused and took a deep breath. "This is like a fantasy. A dream come true."

LeAnn's first hour in Saigon—first photo there. Mitch—her future son—in background.

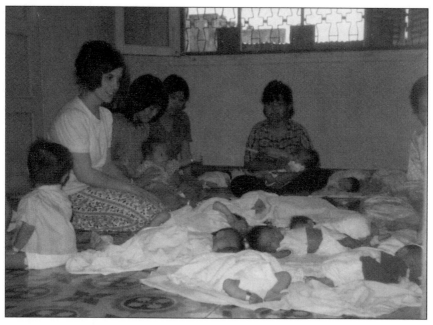

Carol with workers at The Center.

Workers at Center working and sleeping with babies.

Workers caring for babies at Center.

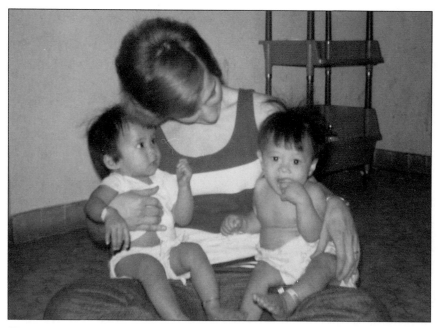

The day LeAnn chose her son! He is on her left knee, "Personality" on her right.

Carol and Thuy.

The girl in the straw hat.

Carol's little friend.

Workers loading babies onto cargo jet in Saigon.

LeAnn in van taking babies to airport.

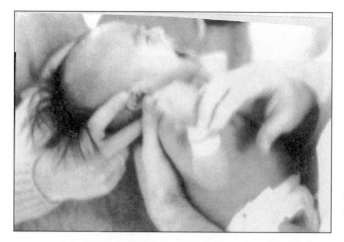

Girl with shaved head.

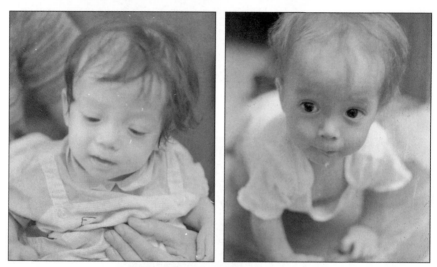

Johnson twins —Christopher, above left, and Anthony, above right.

Mai before leaving Vietnam.

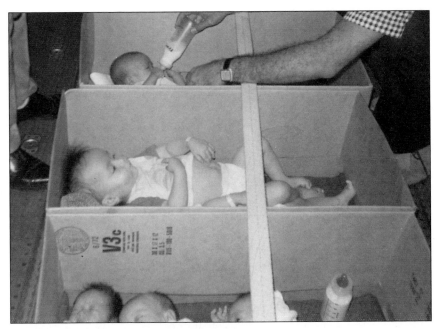

Bringing babies out of Saigon, 3 to a box.

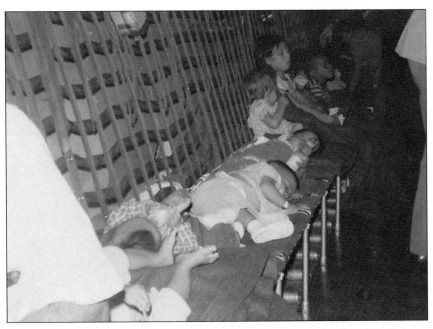

Toddlers and older kids on benches on sides of cargo jet leaving Saigon.

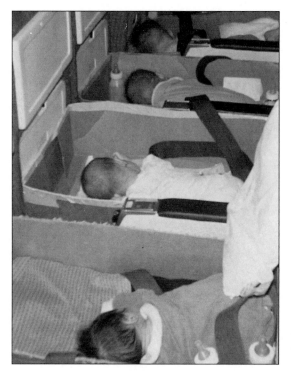

Babies leaving Clark
Air Force Base.

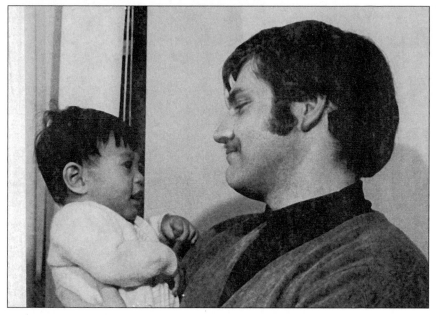

Mitchell meeting his daddy.

Chapter Ten

One of the last things I had told Angela and Christie was that our baby wasn't ready yet and wouldn't be coming home with me. Now, in this world of incredible events, something even more incredible was about to happen.

I opened the door and we entered a room filled with babies. Babies on blankets and mats. Babies in boxes and baskets and bassinets and cribs.

"Carol, how will I ever choose? There are 110 babies here now."

"Some are girls," she offered. "That should limit your selection some."

The memory of the death that morning crept into my mind. "What if I pick one that isn't healthy and doesn't survive the trip?" And there was always the possibility that the baby I chose would have a disability or be mentally handicapped.

When we first looked into adoption we had considered handicapped children. Since we already had two birth children we were only eligible for a hard-to-place child. Because I was a nurse and Mark worked with handicapped kids at the University we thought we would be well qualified and knew we'd love the child unconditionally. After much discussion, though, we feared the reality of that commitment threatened our time and resources with Angela and Christie and we made the decision to adopt a different hard-to-place child. That's when we made application through FCVN.

One baby in a white T-shirt and diaper looked at me with bright eyes. I sat cross-legged on the floor with him on my lap. He seemed to be about nine months old and responded to my words with cute facial expressions and animation. I saw lots of teeth as he smiled and toddled around me and I knew he was older than I had first surmised. He giggled and clapped his hands.

"We should name you Personality," I said. Then I noticed he was wearing a name bracelet on his ankle. This baby had already been assigned to a family in Denver. Well, I thought, feeling disappointment rising in my throat, that family is mighty lucky.

Another child caught my eye as he pulled himself to his feet beside a wooden crib. We watched with amusement as he tugged at the toes of the baby sleeping inside and then dropped back to his hands and knees and began crawling to us. I met him halfway across the room and picked him up. He wore only a diaper and his soft, round tummy bulged over its rim. He looked at me and smiled brightly, revealing chubby cheeks and deep dimples. As I hugged him he nestled his head into my shoulder.

"Maybe you'll be our son," I whispered. He pulled back, staring into my eyes, still smiling. I carried him around the room, looking at each infant, touching them, talking to them. The baby in my arms babbled, smiled, and continued to cuddle. I couldn't bring myself to put him down as we went upstairs where the floor was carpeted with more babies. The hallway was like a megaphone, blasting the sounds of chattering workers and crying babies.

"Let me hold him," Carol coaxed, "while you look at the others." The couch against the wall held a half-dozen fussy infants side by side. I picked up each of them. Most seemed stiff and unresponsive. How sad that cuddling could be unfamiliar to them. I weaved my way to the blanket at the end of the room and sat caressing the infants there. As I cradled one in my arms, I could feel the bones of his spine press against my skin. Another's eyes looked glazed and motionless. Sorrow gripped me.

The little boy Carol had been carrying for me patted my arm. As I turned to look, he reached his chubby arms out to me. Taking him from her, I snuggled him close. Someone had loved him very much.

Downstairs, we meandered from mat to crib looking at all the infants again. I wished I could adopt them all. But I knew there were long waiting lists at the Denver headquarters of hundreds of families who had completed the tedious, time-consuming application process. Each of these precious orphans would have immediate homes carefully selected for them.

"How do I choose?" I asked myself as much as Carol. The baby boy in my arms answered by patting my face. "I wish Mark were here."

I allowed myself to turn my full attention to the child I held, waving my hands in front of his face to check his eyes. He blinked and flashed his dimples.

I snapped my fingers by his ears to test his hearing. He turned his head, giggled, and grabbed at my hands.

Then I sat on the floor slowly rocking him back and forth in my arms. I whispered a prayer for the decision I was about to make, a decision that would affect many lives. The baby snuggled into the hollow of my neck, reassuring me that the choice I was about to make was the right one. I could feel his shallow breath and tender skin as he embraced me.

I recalled all the data we had collected, all the letters of references from friends, bankers and employers, all the interviews with the social workers.

It had all been worth it for this moment.

We rocked in silence and cuddled. Then, with immense joy, I walked back through the nursery door to the office.

"Meet our son, Mitchell Thieman," I announced, hardly believing my own words. Everyone gathered around and embraced us. I looked at Mitchell's puzzled face then held him closer. Cherie brought a name tag and I eagerly scrawled "Reserve for Mark Thieman" on it and placed it on his ankle. Joyful tears streamed down my cheeks. For a moment all my fears were gone. I no longer wondered why I had been driven to make this journey. "This is why God sent me to Vietnam," I whispered.

I had been sent to choose a son.

Or had he chosen me?

Chapter Eleven

Carol was relentless in her attempts to call home. At noon the call she placed to Iowa City earlier that day was returned. It was about midnight in Iowa and Sally, the woman who was baby-sitting Chris and Chad, had been asleep. She said that the Associated Press had contacted them earlier, telling that Carol was not among those in the plane crash.

"A part of me was disappointed that I didn't get to talk with Al," she told me. Yet she admitted another part was relieved.

The staff gathered on the second story veranda for lunch. Carol talked cheerfully about her conversation with Sally. I was buoyed by the joy of choosing our son. Looking past the beautiful green palm trees and flowers, we could see the shabby wooden buildings across the street. Bullets had shattered the windows.

"You know," Ross began with a devilish grin, "I hear those windows were blown out your first night here when the Vietcong invaded the Center. Surely you remember that battle!"

"Hey, we were convinced!" I tried to sound defensive.

"Close enough for me!" added Carol and we laughed again at our misadventures.

As we ate chicken noodle soup my mind flashed to the chicken carcasses that hung in the booths of the street vendors. I struggled to block the sight from my mind. The Vietnamese cook had served the meal proudly and smiled as her guests consumed it.

"It's delicious," Carol complimented.

"Ga-to," the cook said, pointing to the chicken.

"Ga-to?" Carol repeated. The woman nodded, a smile unfolding on her wrinkled face.

She served us tiny bananas. I had never seen them so small. "Thank you."

"Su-cam-ta," she responded, translating my English into Vietnamese.

"Su-cam-ta," I repeated. She beamed.

One worker placed her straw hat on Carol's head. "Non," she said, tapping the hat with her fingertips.

"Non," Carol echoed, dancing around the table as everyone laughed together.

I was surprised when Cherie suggested then would be a good time to go on another mission in Saigon, one I had mentioned to her days earlier. With the stress of the crash and the pressures of the impending airlift, I was impressed Cherie had remembered.

Our family had been introduced to a Vietnamese exchange student who was attending high school in Iowa City. Tong had joined us for dinner a few times and spoke English well. He was understandably worried about his family still living in Saigon and the effects of the war on their lives. Because of the political status of his country, he had not received much mail and was concerned about the improbability of his returning here. On his last visit with us he had given me a handwritten note to deliver to his family in Saigon. There seemed to be no end to Cherie's compassion as she offered to have Ross accompany me in the van to find the home of Tong's sisters. I felt a bit guilty about leaving the work at the Center to embark on a personal outing of uncertain results.

Shi, a young native staff member about Ross' age, was the driver on the trip. He spoke in perfect English of his dream to go to America someday. He was doubtful he would get government clearance to go with the babylift.

"And I don't have enough money to buy my way out."

"I keep hearing that you can buy your way out of Vietnam. I've never understood that," I said eager for an opportunity to talk to a native.

He explained that the Vietnamese government, hoping to avert a mass exodus, banned travel abroad and passports were only issued for "special cases." To qualify for that category, a bribe of $2,000 dollars was needed. Even so, the passport office was crammed with applicants. On city streets, he said, it was not uncommon to see people selling precious family heirlooms to raise money for tickets out of the country.

"Last month Air Vietnam was flying one flight a day from other towns to Saigon for the cost of $9.50. Now they are flying five flights a day and tickets are going for as much as $300 on the black market. Even guards at the airport entrance take bribes. So you see why I cannot afford to leave."

"But I thought there were some so-called priority evacuations for Vietnamese with proven U.S. connections," said Ross with a note of hope.

"Your government promises that," he said with disgust, "but how are we to trust them? They have promised many things."

He told accounts of hundreds of people stampeding the American Consulate hoping to be a "special case" for approved evacuation.

"I read that mimeographed consulate passes were photocopied and forgeries were passed on or sold to close friends or relatives," Ross added, verifying his story. "Things are a zoo at the embassy! Even though they downplay the seriousness of the situation here, there are 6,000 Americans in Saigon trying to get permission to leave now too, before the panic sets in." He added that many Americans feared they could become scapegoats for the anger and frustration welling up in the South Vietnamese. "Many think we let them down," he added, shaking his head sadly.

Our driver concluded the conversation. "My family left the North twenty years ago with millions of other refugees and came south to escape the communism. Where do we go now? We are at the bottom and can go no further."

We rode in silence.

He maneuvered the van confidently through the noisy, chaotic streets of the downtown area. This part of the city was poorer, crowded with pushcarts, bicycles, beggars, shine boys, and wounded war veterans. A three-wheeled taxi designed to carry eight small people passed carrying sixteen. A wheel fell off the axle and everyone abandoned the taxi in the middle of the crowded street.

In contrast to the loud, exciting places I'd seen earlier, this area seemed depressed and bleak. Dirty, barefoot children in torn clothes played alongside the cluttered streets. Families sat on straw mats on the asphalt eating bowls of rice. A small kettle sat on top of a tiny clump of burning sticks.

When we passed a shot-up street sign, Ross looked back at me, winked, and muffled a laugh with his hand.

Because Tong had written the address in Vietnamese, we had difficulty locating the house. Finally the van wound into a quieter neighborhood and came to a stop at what seemed to be the correct address. A black wrought-iron fence and gate was locked in front of the attractive brick home that sat well back from the street. I pulled a cord at the gate which I assumed was a call bell of sorts. There was no answer. I pulled it a second time. Still no one came. I stood, waiting nervously, for several minutes while Ross and the driver watched from the van. I was sad and frustrated to think I was so near Tong's family but would have to tell him I had been unsuccessful in delivering the letter. Finally a teenage girl peered from the front door, then slowly exited and approached me. Her short, black hair framed her beautiful face with its fair complexion and brown eyes. She seemed frightened of me as I spoke to her in English and she shook her head several times. I repeated her brother's name and finally handed her the letter. Slowly the girl walked to the house and I returned to the van feeling confused and still frustrated about the questionable success of the venture.

Arrangements had been made for Carol and Ross and me to go to the American Officer's Club that night to meet Steve and Carol Johnson for dinner. Carol and I had met them the day of the crash when they were among those who had come to the Center to support their grieving friends. I was uncomfortable about leaving Mitchell for the evening. As his mom, I wanted to be the one to cuddle him and rock him to sleep in my arms. Everyone assured me, though, that the workers would take good care of him. They reminded me that Cherie was pleased to have been able to make these reservations for us as a thank-you for our efforts.

We tried to coax Cherie to join us but she refused to leave her pressing duties. There was hope that the FCVN airlift would be the next day. We felt a little guilty ourselves at the thought of leaving to have fun while she continued to work.

Cherie was a woman driven by a singular passion: to save the babies. While others did individual tasks that she had assigned, she had the tremendous responsibility of the overall plan. I could only begin to guess at the depth and complexity of emotions with which she must have struggled as she made preparations for herself and so many others to leave the land she'd grown to love. She was already without her husband and anticipating splitting the family further by sending more of her kids to the States as soon as possible.

We were more than touched that in the midst of her hectic schedule, she had arranged for us to have an evening out with new friends. It seemed only right to go.

Several years earlier Steve Johnson had been working as a communication specialist for the army in Saigon when he met Carol Kim, a beautiful Vietnamese singing star. He returned as a civilian to do the same work for ITT and to continue his volunteer work for FCVN. He was Cherie's communication link to Denver and, because he had U.S. postal priority, all mail went through him. On weekends he transported supplies and children all over the country. He was in the process of adopting Amerasian twin boys when he married Carol Kim who had a ten-year-old son. She would be singing tonight at the restaurant. It would be a night of good-byes if the rumored airlift materialized for the following day. Hopefully, along with the infants, Carol and I would be taking the three Johnson boys and four of Cherie's children back to the States with us.

There was a spirit of festivity in the American Officer's Club, a stark wood-paneled room filled with wooden tables and chairs. The three of us found Steve sitting at a long table and he smiled proudly as he nodded toward his wife Carol singing on the small stage at the end of the room. The pianist swayed with her emotion while accompanying her on the old upright piano as she sang a sad American melody. Her straight black hair flowed over the shoulders of her shapely body as she crooned the lonely song.

When the song was over, she gave a small curtsy and joined us at the table where she sat next to Steve. He looked like an "all American boy" with sandy-brown hair and a slim build. His light-blue eyes were deep set and reflected sorrow as he spoke of sending his sons to the States without him. He had a gentle manner and affectionately explained that he would be trying to obtain passage out of Vietnam as soon as possible for his wife. It would be more difficult because she was a Vietnamese citizen.

His wife Carol talked with us for a while before returning to the stage. The pain she felt at the prospect of saying good-bye to her children the next day was all too obvious. Her tears flowed as she sang a melancholy tune. I thought of my own pain of parting with Angela and Christie only a few days earlier. I couldn't imagine the agony she felt not knowing when she'd be with her sons again.

Chapter Eleven

An American dinner of baked potatoes, steak, and salad was served. Carol reminded me of the warnings given us by the Americans in Manila not to eat fresh fruits and vegetables. Ross assured us, however, that all the food served here was brought from the United States and would be safe. I, in my usual trusting way, enjoyed the greens. Carol, in her usual cautious manner, declined.

"To Mitchell!" Ross shouted as he raised his glass and beamed his lively smile.

"To Mitchell!" the group chorused as our glasses clinked together. I blushed some, still hardly believing that we really had a son.

Since I had eaten very little for two days, the food tasted good and in spite of the sadness, there was talking and light-hearted teasing.

Still, the cloud of worry about the approaching war cast a shadow on the fun of the evening.

"In Iowa we only had to watch the evening news or pick up the daily newspaper to know what was happening with the war. Now here we are on the fringes of it and I have no idea how close it is. That feels real scary," I admitted.

"It's real close," is all Steve would say. The tortured look on his wife's face confirmed that fact. For an instant we all sat in uncomfortable, solemn silence.

Then, in an apparent attempt to suppress the pain and change the mood, Carol went back on stage—this time belting out, "Won't You Come Home Bill Bailey," in her throatiest voice. We all clapped our hands and howled. Ross put his fingers to his mouth to create a shrieking whistle.

"It's hard to believe we're in Vietnam," I shouted above the music. This was a scene out of America.

But the reality of the war returned as Ross warned, "We need to leave now if we're to get back by the 10 o'clock curfew." Abruptly the festivities ended to comply with the strictly enforced law. We all hugged good-bye and made plans to meet before the airlift which was expected the next day. Ross drove quickly through the nearly abandoned streets.

"Even the toughest street boys, prostitutes, and soup vendors get off the streets an hour before curfew. They're all afraid of the communists."

Carol's young friend greeted her at the door as we entered the Center and found Cherie and Thuy still at work. The partyers shared the events of our evening and Cherie listened with interest as we recalled the fun.

I tiptoed into the nursery to check on Mitchell, where he slept next to a worker. I touched his cheek, still struggling with the reality that he was ours. The worker stirred so I crept quietly back to join the group in the office.

"Thuy may have a marriage proposal," Cherie teased.

Thuy blushed shyly. Cherie explained it wasn't uncommon for American men to marry Vietnamese women to facilitate their entry into the United States.

"Is that legal?" we asked yet again.

"There is no way they can prove it wasn't a marriage made in heaven," Cherie said wryly. "We've got other means to try first, though. Remember, we don't make the rules."

"We just have to find a way to comply with them." I completed her phrase for her. Thuy looked worried.

"After all you've done, we'll get you out with us . . . one way or another." Cherie turned her back to Thuy and exchanged a fretful look with Ross.

Knowing the years Thuy had spent going to college in the United States and appreciating all her work for FCVN, it seemed unjust that she would have to stay behind. I tried to erase from my mind the horrible stories of torture and death that were predicted for those nationals who had aided the Americans. One news report estimated as many as 200,000 Vietnamese might be killed or imprisoned by the communists for that reason. We couldn't let that happen to Thuy.

"We'll get you out," Cherie repeated with a wink.

I held my belly and moaned slightly. "I guess I ate too much. I have a real stomachache."

Chapter Eleven

The Center, filled with over 100 babies and dozens of workers, had just two bathrooms. I excused myself and went to the closest one where my cramping increased and explosive diarrhea began. As everyone else prepared for bed, I grew more ill. I began to change but rushed immediately back to the bathroom. It was occupied so I ran to the one in the Clark's quarters, which was also being used. The abdominal pain increased as I lay on the floor outside the door fearing my bowels would explode. The occupant must have heard my moaning and quickly exited. I entered the bathroom for what would be only one of many times that night.

I slept fitfully on the office floor. The increasing pains in my belly woke me and I ran to the toilet over and over again. I tried to scurry quietly past the sleeping workers and babies. When the bathroom was occupied, I lay on the floor outside the door. The cool tile soothed my burning face. The pains increased, reminding me of the labor pains of childbirth. I tried not to moan aloud as I curled in a ball on the floor, drifting in and out of sleep.

Chapter Twelve

Sounds of babies fussing and cooing and the chatter of the workers came from the nursery next door. I woke, still clutching my abdomen.

"How are you feeling?" Carol asked.

"Like I've been hit in the stomach with fists." I forced a grin. "You were right. I shouldn't have eaten the salad."

Carol just smiled, probably stifling the urge to say I told you so. "Maybe you need to rest today."

I insisted that the worst of the illness was surely over and felt that the excitement of the day would give me the strength I needed to help with final preparations. I hoped that taking a shower would help, but first I wanted to see my son.

A worker sat on the mat next to him feeding him rice and chopped vegetables for breakfast. Quite a change from the strained baby food most babies ate in the U.S.

"Hi, Buddy." I held my arms out and he reached for me. There were those dimples again. I recognized the worker as one who spoke a little English and asked if the children only ate rice. She boasted that although rice was eaten at most meals, it usually had ground vegetables or fish in it for good nutrition.

It was wonderful just to hold Mitchell in my arms. I didn't

want to put him down, let alone leave him to do the work that day. I whispered about the plans to leave for his new home soon and told him about his loving daddy and sisters waiting.

Already I loved him.

The upstairs shower stall amused me. The shower head came from the middle of the wall only about three feet from the floor. Crouching to let the water stream over me, I wondered how others used that setup. As I dried myself I realized my body was thinner and admitted to myself that I felt as puny as I looked. I joined Carol in the kitchen for french bread and cola, our usual breakfast. Our conversation about plans to leave Saigon that day renewed my energy and enthusiasm. The time on my watch prompted us to imagine what our families were doing then. We were homesick and gleamed at the prospect of being with them in a few days.

"I'll never again take for granted the everyday things in the United States," Carol teased. "Like taking a shower and doing my hair and eating breakfast."

"And sharing a bathroom with only three people!" I added, recalling my past night's experience.

Cherie directed us to the nursery where we were to make a final check that each infant had ankle and wrist identification bracelets.

One of the Vietnamese nurses approached us. In broken English she expressed her dream to take her three children to the United States someday. "I'm so scared here." The expression on her face underscored that fear.

Three doctors arrived to make final rounds in the nursery to make certain that each baby was medically stable enough to leave. Cherie assisted them as they went crib by crib. It was decided that two of the babies, who had been named Maggie and Joanie, were not well enough to travel and would be taken to the Saigon hospital instead.

"But, Cherie, if they don't leave now, they may never get out," Carol protested kindly.

"But if they go on the flight, they may not live. We can't take that risk."

I looked at the limp, frail bodies in the cribs and knew she was right. It was a common belief that when Saigon fell to the communists the Amerasian children might be killed. There were no good choices. Cherie reiterated her plans to bring more babies out after this flight and assured us that she'd do everything possible to have these two babies among them.

Deep inside I wondered if Maggie and Joanie would ever know full health or freedom.

"Dr. Cuong says *this* little one will make the trip." Cherie smiled as she picked up a tiny baby girl barely newborn size. Half of her head had been shaved while the rest was covered with thick black hair four inches long. Her bracelet said she was five months old. "Her story is a little like yours, LeAnn," Cherie said as she kissed the red IV sites on the shaved stubble. "Her assigned parents, Sally and Paul, were here last month as escorts and, like you, were drawn to this one special child. When they saw her at the orphanage, Paul picked her up and tickled her feet. When she gave him a big grin the nun exclaimed, 'This is the first time this baby has smiled!' Sally and Paul said they knew then that God had sent them here to find her. Her adoption paperwork wasn't complete yet, so they couldn't take her with them. They were heartbroken to leave her behind."

"We're outta here!" Ross nearly leapt into the room. "We leave this afternoon!" He motioned to the 150 children and infants at the Center, on the floors, in infant seats, clothes baskets, cribs, and boxes. "Pack up!" He ordered with a laugh.

Workers in every room began dressing the babies for their journeys. Infants who had been in diapers or sleepers were now dressed in their Sunday best. It was incredible to see them in the shorts, shirts, and ruffly dresses we had sent from Iowa.

The women who had previously cared for them so merrily now cried openly as they dressed them one last time. Many of the foster mothers who had come to help with the work at the Center wept as they prepared to relinquish the baby they had cared for as their own. We hugged many sorrowing women, barely able to imagine their feelings.

"Not only are we taking away the babies, we're taking away their purpose," Carol's voice quaked.

Then she spotted the beautiful, silent little girl the nuns had brought, still wearing the wide-brimmed straw hat. The cold, blank stare presented a mask of bravery. Her jaw, usually firmly set to forbid any expression on her lips, began to quiver. Carol silently knelt beside her. As the child glared into Carol's face, a single tear appeared in the corner of her eye. Suddenly the horror and heartache the child had seen could be denied no more. She threw her arms around Carol's neck and her body gave way to convulsive sobs. There was nothing Carol could do but hold her as she wept.

In the kitchen, workers were preparing hundreds of glass bottles of formula. When I noticed each was boiling hot, I cautioned the worker at the stove. In broken English she reported that it had been done deliberately, figuring that they would cool and be just the right temperature by the time we boarded the plane. She smiled proudly at what she thought was an ingenious idea.

I hoped she was right.

The city bus that was to transport the babies to the airport was too large to maneuver the narrow streets near the Center so it was parked several blocks away on a main street. Carol and I began loading babies into smaller vans to be taken to the city bus. I sat inside and placed babies all around me as I had done in the previous trip to the Australian flight.

That had been before the crash.

My mouth went dry with fear and I jostled the baby in my arms. I couldn't help but wonder about the fate of the flight we were about to take. Would it too be bombed or sabotaged? My worry was interrupted by the sounds of more babies crying and the pressures of the task at hand.

As Carol carried a baby from the Center to the van, a Vietnamese woman in a head scarf touched her arm to get her attention. She pointed to a boy, probably about eight years old, sitting next to the window in the van. His frightened eyes were moist as he stared out the window at her. She tapped the left side of her chest and said, "Not forget me."

He had a picture of her in his pocket.

Her eyes, sad and dark, carried a burden of a mother giving up her child.

As Carol handed me the baby in her arms, she described the encounter and the anguished look on the woman's face.

"Do you think she actually gave up her son?" she choked. "I can't help thinking about Chris and Chad. I can't imagine what she's going through. I don't want to believe it." If it were true it would be the greatest maternal sacrifice.

When asked, these women denied that the children were theirs, Cherie said. Each had to sign a release form swearing the child was an orphan.

Such a sacrifice made to save the life of the child.

With nearly a dozen babies around me, I instructed Ross to begin driving to the waiting city bus. The infants were too crowded to roll around as it crept through the narrow streets. Once at the main thoroughfare, we carried them to the larger bus and placed them three on a seat. A couple of women from the center stayed with them as Carol and I returned with the van to the Center for repeat loads.

"What's going on there?" I nodded toward where Cherie stood near the front door. A priest seemed to be pleading with her as she listened compassionately.

"That priest is hoping Cherie can help him get his orphans out too," Thuy answered shaking her head dismally.

"What does Cherie say?"

"She'll do everything she can."

Each seat on the city bus was full. It was time to take the first of several loads of children to the airport.

Every baby on every seat was crying. We had placed them three or four to a seat with their heads against the seat back to prevent them from rolling forward when the bus slowed or stopped. They each looked so cute in their frills and fancy clothes, but their little arms and legs were flailing as they screamed. The task of transporting them safely seemed monumental.

Carol, Ross, and I placed ourselves in the aisles to watch over the babies as the bus slowly inched its way to the airport. The noise and motion of the bus soothed some of the crying infants but the three of us still had to shout to be heard above the din. We stretched our arms and legs to guard the babies from falling and began to laugh as we looked at each other balancing nearly spread eagle trying to steady the precious cargo.

"I think I saw this on Laurel and Hardy once," I shouted. Carol and Ross laughed in spite of the stress of stabilizing the little bodies. I knew, certainly, that there was no time to make better accommodations for transportation. President Thieu had set a time and date for their departure and it was FCVN's problem to meet that deadline. His seemingly deliberate efforts to make the airlift fail only served to strengthen our conviction to make it succeed.

There were several older children on the bus and they tended to the babies placed beside them on the seat. A little girl with straight black hair patted the backs of the three babies beside her as she cooed to them in Vietnamese. I listened as another boy sang native songs while rocking the baby whimpering in his arms. The bus driver turned the corners at a snail's pace as we moved from seat to seat to insure the safety of each baby.

It seemed like hours passed before we arrived at the gates

of the airport. The guard stopped the bus and the driver motioned for Ross to come forward to speak to him. Ross began to argue in his broken Vietnamese dialect. He turned to us and shouted, "President Thieu has canceled our flight. We have to wait for clearance."

Carol and I groaned in unison.

Ross turned back to the guard. "We can't just wait in this bus with all these babies. It's 95 degrees outside and even hotter in here!" The babies began to wail even louder since the rocking motion had stopped.

"These babies are going to lose a lot of fluid in these tears," Carol shouted, "and the heat will probably cause diarrhea which will make them dehydrate for sure!" She scrambled to find the boxes packed with formula. "It's still boiling hot! Now what'll we do?"

Idling in the sun, the bus became an instant oven. We began picking up one baby, then another, in a frenetic effort to comfort as many as possible while Ross continued to argue with the guard. Perspiration plastered our clothes to us and sweat dripped from our faces.

As the air inside the bus grew hotter, the little ones grew more frantic. Stroking their damp hair, I blew gently into their faces and waved a diaper as a fan. How sadly ironic that we had cases of formula, but nothing to feed the squalling cargo. The baby with the shaved head lay on the seat wet from her own tears and sweat.

Slowly the bus began to inch forward through the opening gates.

"They're letting us use the Quonset huts while we wait for this mess to get straightened out," Ross yelled, sounding relieved.

"Maybe we should go back to the Center in the meantime so we can take better care of these babies," Carol called back. "They won't be able to take much more of this."

"No way!" Ross bellowed. "That's just what they want us to do. We are not leaving until the babies are on that plane!"

117

Ross drove across the tarmac to a series of three metal Quonset huts. As soon as we came to a halt, we began unloading the precious cargo. The babies' pretty clothes clung to their sweaty little bodies as they continued to cry.

I watched as a little passenger, about five years old, struggled to carry the infant he had been tending. As the tiny body slid down in his arms, his face grimaced and his muscles tightened as he clutched the baby closer. The words to the theme song from the slide show I had presented so many times came to life . . . *"He ain't heavy . . . he's my brother."* I blinked back the tears. How sad that he had to carry one so small. How wonderful that he would.

The old building was filthy inside. Cobwebs and dust hung from the metal walls. The infants were placed in boxes or on blankets on the dirty concrete floor. The small windows near the ceiling were so dirty that light could barely filter through. Other civilians waiting to serve as escorts on the outgoing flight came inside to help.

The sounds of the crying echoed off the sides of the tin walls. A water fountain was spotted against one wall and we eagerly ran each bottle of formula under the stream to cool it enough for the babies to drink. It was bedlam as everyone shouted and scurried among the tiny crowd trying to feed four or five babies at a time.

Several American reporters were covering the airport. When they heard about the babies, they descended on the hut, pushing closer to take pictures while scribbling furiously on note pads. One, a tall, plump, brown-haired woman with big, dark glasses began taking charge and shouting instructions to the volunteers. She also loudly speculated on what would happen if President Thieu would not let the babies out. Some workers obviously resented her and scowled at her comments.

"We don't need negativity now!" I hollered to the reporter above the reverberation. "We need all the positive help we can get!"

Chapter Twelve

In a huff, she began to feed a baby.

"What *will* happen if the president refuses to let the babies leave?" someone asked.

"Will *any* of us ever get out of Saigon?"

"If so, they'd better hurry and okay the airlift before this whole country falls!"

"Where is more cool formula? This stuff is still too hot!"

Ross returned with the latest word from airport officials. "President Thieu now says he'll let this plane—but *only* this one planeload of orphans leave."

Carol and Ross had planned to stay with this load of children and I was to return to the Center and get Mitchell and the remaining infants.

"What about the rest of the babies?" I refused to hear his message.

Ross held up his finger. "One planeload. That's all they'll say."

I was frantic. What should I do?

"You take my place on this flight," Ross insisted.

"I can't!" I was shaking with panic. "I have to go get Mitchell. I can't leave without him!" Ross put his arm around me and I buried my face in his sweat-stained shirt.

Then he placed one hand on each of my shoulders and fixed his eyes on mine.

"You leave now with Carol. Get out while you can. I promise you, I will get Mitch out and bring him to you in Iowa City."

"But what if you don't get out? You said yourself that no more babies are going to be allowed to leave."

"I will. I promise you." Ross's voiced cracked.

I paused, rubbing moisture from my face with the back of my hand, and considered his idea. In my mind I felt Mark's embrace and saw my daughters' faces.

Then I made one of the most difficult decisions of my life.

"I won't leave without him," I said.

The city bus was ready to return to the Center where it

was supposed to have picked up the second load of children. Realizing that I was steadfast in my decision, Ross suggested there was a slight chance that I could go to the Center, get Mitchell, and return to the airport before the plane took off. He said he would do all he could to hold the flight, but he and I both knew he would be powerless to do so.

Ross explained the plan to the bus driver. I climbed the bus stairs two at a time and immediately turned and jumped out again.

I had to find Carol.

She was sitting amidst the pandemonium inside the Quonset hut rocking two babies in her lap and one on her shoulder. I quickly told her of my plan to try and retrieve Mitchell and get back in time to leave with her. The worry in her eyes was not expressed in her voice as she said, "Hurry. After all we've been through together, we can't get separated now."

I hugged her tight, forced a smile, and ran to board the bus.

I was not only leaving her but, with this decision, possibly everything I ever loved.

The same bus that crept so slowly en route to the airport now sped rapidly, almost recklessly, back to the Center with me as its only passenger. The crowded streets, the hundreds of weaving bicycles, the laneless convoy of cars all angered me as the bus honked and jerked through the snarled traffic.

Why couldn't they hurry?

Why couldn't they clear a path?

Didn't they know that this was literally a matter of life and death?

Already I couldn't imagine my life without Mitchell.

Finally the driver stopped the bus on the main street, opened the door, smiled, and pointed down the narrow street ahead. I raced off the bus and ran down the dirt streets toward the Center.

Although breathless, as I ran I began to pray out loud.

"Please, God, please let me leave with my son."

Chapter Twelve

The strap of my sandal broke and the shoe flopped wildly against my ankle as I ran. Finally, I grabbed it without breaking my stride, clenched it in my hand, and ran with one bare foot as fast as I could.

My side ached fiercely as I pushed harder. The Center was in sight. A numbness and burning fired through my legs. Panting and puffing, I ran through the courtyard gates, up the steps, and into the office. Cherie looked up, startled.

I wheezed, hardly able to speak. "Only one flight out. I have to get Mitchell!"

Cherie interrupted me. "I know, I know," she said easing me into a chair. "I just got off the phone. The plane will wait for you."

I beamed a smile while gasping for breath.

Thank You, God!

She waited for me to catch my wind before she continued. Officials had notified her that the flight would wait for additional babies and a second flight was approved to leave also.

Still panting, I located Mitchell in the adjoining room waiting with the other babies. He wore a white shirt and red checkered playsuit, and he smiled when I picked him up and held him close.

"I'll never leave you again," I whispered. "I won't let you out of my sight until we're home."

Quickly, the workers assisted Cherie, Thuy, and me in the loading of more babies into the van then onto the waiting city bus. After the last of the babies was loaded they helped us on the frenzied bus ride to the airport.

The bus entered the air base without interruption this time and pulled alongside a U.S. Air Force cargo jet.

"All right!" Ross shouted as he watched Mitch and me get off the bus. "See, I told you I'd hold the plane!" he boasted as he and Carol ran to embrace us.

U.S. Air Force personnel came over to help.

"Boy, are we glad to see you!" Carol gleamed. "You make me feel closer to home."

Everyone began carrying the infants on board. Excitement and happiness seemed to energize the Vietnamese workers. This was the moment that they had worked for so hard and so long.

My throat felt tight as I anticipated boarding the plane. I held Mitchell as the others completed the loading of the orphans. When the final children were aboard, we escorts turned to bid the workers and staff good-bye. Virtually all of the loyal, loving workers began to cry. I sensed their tears were partly of joy for the babies, partly out of a sense of loss, and possibly out of fear for their own safety. Thuy hugged Carol, Ross, Sister, and me good-bye and I wondered if we'd ever see her again.

One of the workers from the Center kissed Carol's hand.

"I give you a symbol of my love. You take our babies to America. They be safe there."

Carol's eyes overflowed.

Then came the final and most difficult good-bye.

How could we leave Cherie?

Yet how could we stay?

"I need to stay and get as many babies out as possible," she said. "Don't worry about me. This is my home. I'll be fine."

One by one Ross, Sister, Carol, and I hugged her and whispered words of affection and support.

"Thank you, thank you," was all I could seem to murmur as she enfolded Mitchell and me in her arms. I knew if I spoke more I wouldn't be able to keep from crying. She didn't need that now.

"Don't wait too long," Ross cautioned, squeezing her hand one last time.

She assured us she would get out of the country before it was too late.

"See you in America!" I managed a smile as I walked backward toward the plane with feelings of sorrow and joy wrestling in my heart.

Chapter Thirteen

Carol and I entered the mammoth cargo jet for what we assumed would be a direct flight to the States. We noticed all but a few seats had been removed and had been replaced by long benches along the sides. Down the center was a row of about twenty cardboard boxes, each approximately two feet square. Two to three babies were lying in each box. A long strap was secured at one end of the plane. From there it was stretched over the boxes, then attached to the other end of the plane to hold the boxes securely in place. Several large, metal trash cans were at each end of the row with food, formula, and supplies for the trip. Toddlers and the older children sat with seatbelts on the long benches . . . bewildered orphans strapped inside a flying boxcar.

We adults were instructed by the captain to find a seat and buckle the seatbelt for takeoff. I sat with Mitchell on my lap in one of the few seats near the cabin. An American man, his Vietnamese wife, and two small children sat next to me. The little boy appeared to be about two years old and had a cleft lip and sores on his forehead. His sister, a year or so older, had a few curlers in her hair and wore a flowered dress. It was easy to tell from their faces that they were afraid and confused.

As the captain prepared for takeoff, the sound of the engine's roar was nearly deafening. A panic came over me. My blood raced and my breath stuck in my chest. Although no words were spoken, each escort must have known what the other was thinking. The last planeload of orphans leaving Saigon for America had blown up shortly after take-off. It was still unknown whether it had been shot down or sabotaged.

In a country seemingly fated for tragedy, even that basic humanitarian mission had ended in doom. It was reported to have been the fourth largest aircraft disaster in history.

Would history repeat itself?

My shaking arms gripped Mitchell close to me. He hugged me back as if to comfort me. The remembered image of the black, fiery cloud refueled the terror I had felt the day the plane had crashed.

I began to say the Lord's Prayer as the plane taxied down the runway. I knew that if I lived through the next five minutes, I would make it home to Iowa. The motion of the plane lulled the infants to near silence. The adults sat statue-like. Only the engine's vengeful roar broke the haunting, threatening stillness.

I felt the plane lift off the ground.

"Our Father who art in heaven...." Mitchell sat quietly on my lap, so trusting and unafraid. I glanced at the eyes of the volunteers around me and thought I saw the same tension and fear I felt. Carol sat diagonally across from me on the bench seat. I remembered her reassurance earlier and her firm belief that no one would shoot down a second plane. Her eyes smiled. "We'll be fine," she mouthed.

Finally the American captain spoke. "We are out of range of the Vietcong. We are safe. We are going home."

Whoops of gladness and relief filled the plane. I continued to pray, almost laughing ... this time in my own words, this time in thanksgiving. My heart was lighter, the weight of fear lifted from my chest and shoulders. I stood Mitchell on my lap to face me.

Chapter Thirteen

"We're going home, son."

Immediately the adults on board unfastened their seatbelts and hastened to tend to the babies. Several helpers were Air Force personnel. Many were Americans taking advantage of the opportunity to return home.

One burly man with salt and pepper hair began changing a diaper. His technique made it evident that it was a new experience for him. He admitted that he had never changed a diaper before and we laughed with him as he did it clumsily.

"His wife was killed in the FFAC crash a few days ago," someone whispered. What great courage he had to volunteer for a similar flight.

The commotion of loading and transporting babies had not allowed time to feed them. Now all ninety were awake and crying simultaneously. The formula was a perfect temperature and we propped countless bottles to rehydrate the crying babies. We discovered we could feed all three babies in a box at the same time by placing them each on their side and propping their bottle on the shoulder of their box-mate. Some sucked the formula down in only minutes, while others needed more help. I cradled a baby girl on my folded legs and coaxed her to drink while using my left hand to feed another baby in the box. The nipple fell from the mouth of the baby in my lap. Clearly she was too weak to suckle. Using both hands, I milked formula from the nipple to drop into her mouth. Although other babies demanded attention, I continued until an ounce was taken.

Older children instinctively joined in the work — and fun — as they held babies and bottles.

"Imagine what's going through the older ones' minds about now," Carol said. "I wonder if they understand where they're going and why."

"Most of them have learned to be afraid of these big military planes," added another male volunteer, "and now they're being put on one and flown away from everything they've ever known and loved."

125

"But what are the choices? Can you imagine what their lives would be like if they stayed in Vietnam?"

I looked at the little girl feeding a baby in her lap. She smiled proudly and I smiled back, trying to reassure her with my expression.

Ross pointed to a sign on the wall of the plane. It read *Freedom Bird.* "Appropriately named," Sister Therese nodded.

"For a lot of reasons," Ross said. "This cargo jet brought prisoners of war out of Vietnam in '73."

As the bottles emptied, we held the babies one at a time to burp them. By draping a diaper over a shoulder, we found we could each burp one baby while propping another's bottle with the other hand. Quickly, one baby was returned to its place in the box and another baby picked up for burping. A few of the men held them as if the were made of blown glass and barely tapped their backs.

"They won't break," teased Carol as she demonstrated the burping maneuver. The fellows laughed and followed suit.

"Oh, yuck! Look at you!" one man exclaimed as he wiped vomit from the back of his companion's shirt.

Ross' hands moved quickly as he expertly diapered, fed, and changed babies.

"You're making us look bad!" another man chortled.

"Experience!" Ross bragged.

The predicted diarrhea became a reality and we changed one diaper after another. The handsome burly man wrinkled his face as he dangled a dirty diaper between his thumb and index finger and took it to the assigned trash can. Sister Therese teased this was likely the most challenging work he had ever done. When he reapplied the diaper he stuck the two adhesive tabs together instead of to the diaper. Everyone laughed as he was reinstructed. The jocularity offered a welcomed change to the continued sounds of crying.

Another bachelor said he felt the experience would qualify him as a good candidate for a husband. We all agreed to write him letters of recommendation.

Before long, the plane smelled of diarrhea and spit-up. The babies who had been so neatly dressed and groomed looked wrinkled and soiled. The volunteers were disheveled, but there was a merriment about it all. It was joyful work.

"London sent a Boeing 707 for 150 orphans," boasted one man with a British accent.

"I heard Australia flew out over 200," another offered.

"I can vouch for that!" Carol attested. "We were there and put some of our babies on that plane."

"The Vietnamese Embassy told me another sixty-three went to Canada and fifty more to West Germany," another lady shouted above the noise.

"And now 100 more!" Ross gloated.

This is what orphan relief was all about.

The efforts people had made for years was paying off.

Our flight attendant had been right. We were a part of a plan that could make a difference in the world.

"As President Ford said when he announced the airlift, 'This is the least we can do,' " said the man whose wife had died.

After nearly three hours of feeding, burping, and changing the babies, we were surprised when the pilot announced that we would stop in the Philippines to refuel. That didn't sound like a problem, but the news that we would be detained for each baby to have a medical checkup caused some complaining.

"Why don't they just let us get to Oakland as soon as possible where the babies can get care?" I muttered to a coworker. I felt a little selfish when I was reminded that some babies could be in critical condition if they were to wait until then.

We all acknowledged that the children's health had priority even over our eagerness to get home.

Chapter Fourteen

The plane made a smooth landing on the runway of Clark Air Force Base. Babies gently bumped against one another as the plane came to a halt. Looking out the windows, we were surprised to see dozens of women on the landing strip obviously here to help with our mission. As the plane came to a halt, the women entered the plane one at a time, each exiting with an infant.

"Where did all you ladies come from?" Carol asked.

"Most of us are military wives," a pretty blonde answered as she took the child from Carol's arms. "It's great to be a part of all this," she added, nodding her head toward the fussing cargo.

One woman approached me to take Mitchell.

"Oh, no you don't," I protested with a laugh.

She smiled politely. "We're under strict instructions to take every baby from the plane. No exceptions, I'm afraid."

I clutched him closer to me. "No. I'm his mom."

The volunteer persisted. "Each baby must be checked, in accordance with the U.S. government's plan." She reached for him again. I gently pushed her hand away.

"You don't understand what I've been through to get him. I almost lost him once. Never again!"

Carol came to convince me to let him go. We escorts were

to be taken to a nice motel, she said, where we could clean up and rest. "Then you can be with him again," she reassured me. Reluctantly, I handed Mitchell to the unknown woman. He didn't seem to oppose the separation though my arms and heart felt empty without him.

Admittedly, I felt weak and my abdominal cramping was increasing.

Carol and I deplaned and walked slowly across the hot pavement of the runway. The air was fresh and less humid, though just as hot as it had been in Saigon. We were ushered into a dimly lit building off the runway where we were greeted by women in American Red Cross uniforms.

They welcomed the escorts warmly and reminded us that they were there to assist us in any way possible. The Red Cross knew that telephone communication was nearly impossible in Saigon, and these workers explained that their primary purpose was to notify our families of our safe arrival in the Philippines. While most of the escorts were delighted, I was not at all sure that it was a good idea. I recalled my agreement with Mark that he would trust I was safe and well unless he heard from the Red Cross.

I knew the panic he would feel if the Red Cross phoned him. I explained this to the Red Cross volunteer, but she convinced me that he would be told in a positive way and the call would give him reassurance.

With hesitation, I gave her my full name, social security number, and home phone number in hopes she was right and the call would give Mark some peace of mind. Carol did the same knowing Al would be relieved to hear about her.

As we drove the streets of the air base the gentle breeze, swaying palm trees, and colorful flowers provided a peaceful setting.

But I didn't feel at peace.

Emotions too powerful to suppress kept surfacing. I wondered how much time it would take for the babies to be checked and I worried how long we would have to stay.

Chapter Fourteen

We escorts were dropped at our motel. Together we walked to find our rooms.

"I know I'm paranoid, Ross, but I still don't feel safe here," I blurted, ashamed of my stubborn fear. "It's suspected that the Vietcong shot down one planeload of orphans. What if they still try to bomb these babies here?"

He listened attentively. Then, with a straight face, he told me that no country would attack such a powerful air base and how little Vietnam would gain from such an offensive.

I assured him I would try to be more confident about my safety, but as I left him my anxiety remained.

Carol said it was a treat to take a long, hot shower.

I welcomed having to share a bathroom with only one other person.

I plopped on the soft bed and stared at the ceiling. No lizards. The fluffy pillow under my head reminded me I had left my coat at the Center. I hoped one of the workers would wear it and remember me. When I changed into clean clothes Carol giggled. The skort, which was shorts with a skirt panel in front, was several inches too big. Neither of us had realized until then how much weight I had lost due to dysentery. I began to laugh with her. It was one of the few articles of clothing I had left to wear and we cackled even louder when we realized that because my sandal had broken, I only had brown suede high-top shoes to coordinate the outfit. We rolled on the beds roaring with laughter, aware that this near hysteric state was a healthy release of tension.

We walked with Ross and Sister Therese to the mess hall. Few people were there as we went through the cafeteria line. We joked about the poor reputation of military food, speculating that was the reason for the small crowd.

As we ate we admitted we felt alone and detached from the orphan activities that had consumed us before. In a way the relaxation felt good, but there was an uncomfortable sense of emptiness and loss.

While Ross gobbled down three helpings, I ate very little

from my supper tray, partly because of my stomachache and partly because I was eager to finish and find Mitchell again.

"Let's go see the babies!" Sister Therese said, breaking the silence.

Instantly we took our trays to the conveyor belt and rushed over to the gymnasium that housed the incoming orphans. It looked to be the size of a football stadium. The accommodations for the babies there were certainly a contrast to those they had known in Saigon. Hundreds of single-bed mattresses lay in neat rows on the floor. Each was covered with a white sheet and had diapers, clean clothes, and small toys stacked neatly on one end. Each child from our flight had his or her own mattress and American volunteer. Hundreds more mattresses lay unoccupied awaiting the arrival of more children. The sounds of laughter, cooing, crying, and adult chatter echoed from the gym walls.

Without warning, Sister Therese started to cry. "Somebody cares for them," she said, blowing her nose and wiping her eyes. "Somebody besides us cares for them!"

Sister Therese, Ross, Carol, and I split up to search for Mitchell. Fear crept over me, as I imagined that somehow he could have been lost. I was amazed by the intense maternal instincts that had already bonded me to him. I marched slowly between the rows of mattresses, rhythmically moving my head from left to right, staring at each baby.

And then, there he was. In the middle of the gym, I found him sitting contentedly on a mattress with his volunteer, an Air Force wife. I told the curly-haired woman he was my son and she looked at me with skepticism. When I called her attention to his name bracelet, she told me how lucky I was to have such a wonderful baby. She said medical doctors had assessed each child and that Mitchell was found to be in great health.

Ross, Carol, and Sister Therese found us and we all listened as the volunteer told us two infants had been hospitalized at the base after the flight. They were expected to do very well, she said, explaining that dehydration and fever were the primary problems. These little ones had no reserve.

My friends went back to the motel while I played with Mitchell for a while. I sat cross-legged, rocking him back and forth. He nestled his head into my neck and breathed softly as I sang some of my favorite lullabies.

The volunteer smiled as she looked on. I complimented her for the tremendous volunteer effort and organization that had gone into coordinating this caretaking. She said the military wives had done the same when the prisoners of war had been released from Vietnam two years earlier.

Yet another cost of war.

The noise and the lights in the gym dimmed. Mitchell had fallen into a sound sleep on my shoulder. I carefully laid him on his tummy on the mattress and covered him with a light blanket. I kissed his smooth, soft cheek. "Good night, Son." I loved how that sounded.

We all met in Ross' room and watched the TV reports of the airlift's arrival at Clark. We wondered if the story had national attention and whether our families had heard anything about it back home. The local news interviews were repetitive and poorly done and we sprawled across the couches and the floor and laughed. Exhaustion took its toll and we took turns dozing off. When someone made another joke the howling was repeated.

It felt so good to laugh again.

I became increasingly lightheaded, weak, and achy and finally excused myself to get some sleep. As I lay in bed my innards roared so loudly that Carol could hear it from her bed and we giggled again.

When we finally settled down, I silently prayed in thanksgiving for my son and our safety. As I finished, a feeling of peace and well-being came over me and I realized that for the first time since the Friends For All Children flight crashed, I believed I would live and return home unharmed. I shared my feelings with Carol as we lay there in the dark.

"Believe me," she said, "I know how it feels to get past the turmoil and into a place of strength."

I nestled my face into the crisp, white pillowcase and let silent tears fall.

Partly grieving the loss of the babies in the crash.

Partly rejoicing in the fact that I was not on board as I had originally plotted to be.

Partly for joy in feeling a life's dream was coming true in adopting a son.

And partly for joy in knowing I would soon be home safe with Mark and the girls.

* * *

In Iowa

"Is this Mr. Thieman?" asked the elderly lady's voice on the phone.

"Yes, who's this?"

"I'm from the American Red Cross . . ."

The pang of pain in his chest seemed to stop his heart.

"What's wrong?" he asked panicking, his heart beating like a drum now.

"Is your wife's name Luanna?" the voice droned.

"No, she's LeAnn!" Mark shouted with annoyance and fear.

"Is her Social Security number 000-55-5555?" she asked again, oblivious to the anxiety the call was causing.

Mark slowly and deliberately spoke each of the correct numbers back to her.

Her voice drawled the message. "We just wanted to tell you that she is safe and well in the Philippines."

His spirit soared.

* * *

Carol and I woke the next morning and smiled at one

134

another. It felt good to be lying on clean sheets in a comfortable—and safe—setting. My first thought was of Mitchell. I hoped that he had also slept well in his foreign surroundings. We eagerly dressed and left to be with him. We packed our suitcases and hauled them along, certain that our flight would depart soon.

We arrived to find the gymnasium wall to wall with babies and volunteers. Other flights from other orphan relief agencies had arrived during the night. Nearly 300 babies were now awake and wanting breakfast. Windows lined the top of the walls around the parameter of the building. The morning sunbeams seemed to fill the room and its people with warmth and brightness. The place roared with sounds of early morning happenings . . . bottle feedings, diaper changings, clothes changings, cooing, and chatter. The crying and commotion was a happy kind of noise, though, as volunteers cheerfully tended the babies. Everyone shared the knowledge that lives were being changed and saved by their efforts.

Mitchell was on the same mat in the same location with a new volunteer. He smiled right away when he saw me and reached his arms out. I hugged him close and kissed his cheeks, which already seemed chubbier. I asked him about his night's sleep and told him how much I loved him. He pulled away from me and looked into my face, as he had done so many times before, as if to say he was listening and understood what I was saying. With a promise that we would be back soon, Carol and I left to meet Ross and Sister Therese for breakfast. They told us our flight would not leave until later that evening. We were instructed to enjoy the day.

"I am so anxious to leave and get home. I don't want to stay and enjoy the day," I complained.

I convinced Carol to come with me to meet the Air Force official who was in charge of the airlift operations at Clark. A tall, slim, balding man in his forties walked toward us and introduced himself.

"What can I do for you ladies?"

I pleaded with him to hasten the preparations, telling him how eager I was to get home.

"We're waiting for a proper plane to arrive to accommodate proper evacuation of all these babies," he explained.

I was only half teasing when I said I was satisfied with the cargo jet that brought us out of Saigon.

"If we'd been left alone we would have been in the States by now," I added. The officer assured us that they were doing all they could and encouraged us to relax and enjoy the facilities at Clark. He praised us for what we'd done already and said we should allow others to do the work now while we rested. Carol seemed pleased with that proposal, but I stubbornly resented the delay.

Realizing, however, that I was ineffective at changing the plans of the U.S. government, I reluctantly agreed to the plans for the day. We stacked our suitcases behind his counter, then joined Ross and Sister Therese on an open-air bus ride to the military PX. My first purchase was a pair of inexpensive thongs. I really did look ridiculous wearing shorts with my brown suede high-tops.

We all chuckled as we pretended to select silly gifts for each other. Ross found the newsstand and picked up a copy of *True Confessions Magazine.* "My picture will be on the front of the next issue," he chided. "I Slept with a Minister's Wife and a Nun," he exclaimed, recalling our joking together in front of the TV in his room the night before.

Sister Therese squealed with laughter. "What would Mother Superior say?"

We leaned on each other to keep from falling over while we laughed too loud. Other shoppers forced a smile and steered clear of us.

Finally we resumed our composure and went on to a gallery and gift area. Carol found a painting of a dark-haired woman with a baby in her arms. The child appeared Asian and reminded us of Mitchell. The salesperson explained that the background board had been painted black and the image had been scratched out by the artist. When we were assured that it could be packaged for safe travel, we each bought one. In the gift shop I bought two little purses made from round coconut shells for Angela and Christie. Faces were painted on the fronts and the lids served as little hats.

"These will be good gifts for their new brother to give them," I told Carol. "But then, they have no idea their new brother is coming." I stroked the painted smiles on the purses. "I hope the girls adjust well. Christie will lose her place as the baby of the family in a hurry. She'll be two in less that two weeks." I imagined her birthday party—now envisioning Mitchell as a part of it.

It would be wonderful.

Next we found a small wooden train with six detachable cars. I bought it as the first present for our son and Carol agreed her boys would enjoy pulling one all around their basement playroom.

We found our way to the package shipping area. It was amazing to watch the young Asian men speedily slashing cardboard with long knives to form boxes of any shape. They packed our items carefully with shredded paper and tied the packages with rope for easier carrying. They suggested we could pay to have things shipped directly to our homes, but we decided it was safer to keep them with us.

New purchases in tow, we went back to the airlift headquarters.

"Where have you been?" the officer in charge asked. "You missed your flight."

"You're kidding, right?" Carol chuckled. I looked behind his counter. Our luggage was gone. He was serious.

"The plans changed unexpectedly and the first flight of babies left for the States about an hour ago."

Anger smoldered inside me. "I would have sat here the entire day if I thought there had been even a glimmer of hope for our leaving! We only left because you told us to!"

Carol tried to calm me down as the officer assured us that

our flight would leave very early the next morning.

Mitchell!

Was he on the plane that just left?

I raced several blocks to the gymnasium. I wished they hadn't taken him from me when we arrived. I wanted him with me . . . forever. "Not again!" I panted as I ran, this time in thongs.

I found him playing on his mattress with a volunteer. He smiled up as if to say, "It's okay, Mom." I hugged him and repeated the vow I had made earlier. I would not leave him again.

Chapter Fifteen

It was barely light when we arrived at the airstrip the next day. We should not have been surprised to learn that the plane would be ready for takeoff later than expected. We skipped breakfast in an attempt to be on time to the airfield and while we waited we grew hungrier. It seemed having to hurry up to wait was the basis of military operation.

We found the same officer in charge giving orders to everyone involved in this leg of the journey.

Carol took a picture of the jet we were about to board and was immediately reprimanded. She had a confused look on her face as she whispered, "Why would anyone care?"

We stepped on board to see the accommodations on the DC-10. They were very different from those we had leaving Saigon. Each seat prepared to hold a baby had the same size cardboard box with holes through which the seat belts would pass. It was explained that an adult volunteer would be in charge of two infants to their left and two across the aisle to their right. Dozens of military wives were eager to fly free to assist with the airlift and visit the U.S.A. as well. We complimented the officer for a job well done in coordinating such a mammoth effort.

A parade of volunteers approached the plane one by one, each with the child they had cared for during our stay. The first baby was carried into a quiet cabin, but by the three hundredth baby and the eightieth escort, it was a reverberating aircraft. Within an hour, each box and seat was filled with clamorous cargo. We were finally ready for takeoff.

The flight to the U.S. proceeded down the runway. I had Mitchell in my arms and three other infants to tend. Sister Therese and the infant we'd nicknamed Personality back in another world sat in front of me. He stood on her lap, looked over the seat and continued to entertain us with his laughter and charm. A second baby in her care had club feet but continued his efforts to stand. Ross sat behind us. Mitchell babbled to him as he shook his hand. Carol was across from me. We shared the excitement of the airlift nearing its final goal.

A flight attendant spoke by microphone from the front of the plane orienting the volunteers to the layout of its facilities, the use of the oxygen masks, and where the infants' supplies were. She said we would stop in Hawaii to refuel.

A chubby, balding, middle-aged man took the microphone and instructed us to wake up all the babies so they would be either sucking on a bottle or crying at the time of takeoff. Though we knew that sometimes babies experienced ear pressure with takeoffs and landings, we found the notion of waking 300 babies absurd!

Most people ignored him.

Frequently he took the microphone and pompously gave commands concerning infant care. The escorts clearly disliked him and his arrogant, show-off ways. Just when we got a baby to sleep, he would again come on the mike to shout instructions. I approached him and tried to tell him in a kind way to sit down and shut up, but he was far too busy playing boss to listen.

And I was far too sick to stand and argue.

My cramping recurred and I made frequent trips to the lavatory, asking Carol to keep an eye on my charges. The restroom hardly had room to turn around inside.

Chapter Fifteen

I felt increasingly dizzy and weak.

I heard a loud knock on the locked door and regained consciousness on the bathroom floor, my body wedged between the toilet and the wall. I had no idea how long I had been unconscious. I walked back to my place, gripping each seat back for support.

"Where have you been for so long?" Carol asked. She looked at me with pity when I told her.

The eight-hour flight to Hawaii went quickly. While escorts busily changed diaper after diaper and fed baby after baby, an Associated Press reporter sat among us typing frantically. The plane's aisles were congested with helpers hustling to get supplies and feedings for their charges. One volunteer rocked a baby with skinny legs in one arm while bottle feeding a baby with a bloated belly in the other. Toddlers and older children clung to their caregivers, seemingly begging for affection. Laughter, chatter, fussing, and crying provided a constant concert.

For a moment, all four of the babies in my care rested quietly at the same time. I reclined my seat and closed my eyes as I enjoyed the weight of Mitchell on my chest and felt his shallow breaths on my neck.

I was overcome with joy and, still, disbelief.

What if I had backed out of my promise to go to Vietnam?

But what if I hadn't gotten out?

An unwelcome flash of my former fear ricocheted through me. Tears stung my eyes.

Then from nowhere I could hear my husband Mark singing the John Denver song he learned just before I left. ". . . *Lady, are you crying? Do the tears belong to me? Did you think our time together was all gone?*"

Unconsciously, I nodded. ". . . *Lady, you've been dreaming, I'm as close as I can be, and I swear to you our time has just begun.*"

I used Mitchell's blanket to dry my face. It was really true.

141

The pilot announced we were approaching Hawaii where we would refuel. Though we couldn't argue with the need to do so, we escorts were not excited about the delay. It couldn't take long to fuel a jet, after all. It was almost night-time and the babies were quieting down. The wait would be tolerable.

Then it was announced that the babies would each be carried off the plane and taken inside the airport during the refueling time. Everyone groaned in unison.

I wondered if this was just another dumb idea conceived by the obnoxious man with the microphone. The attendant assured me that it was not, that the doctor on board had determined that a few of the babies needed to be examined to see if they were well enough to continue the trip.

Again I felt embarrassed by my selfish determination to rush home.

The plane landed and we learned that hundreds of volunteers would enter the back of the plane single-file, take a baby, and exit the front. It sounded like a more organized version of the plan used when we landed in the Philippines.

The process took nearly two hours.

When the volunteer came to take Mitchell from me, I explained that he was my son and that I would take charge of him. She insisted that she was following government orders and that he was to go with her.

I relentlessly attempted to enforce the vow I'd made several times before. Feeling weary, I choked back tears and held him tighter as I insisted that he would stay with me this time. The flight attendant intervened and suggested that things would go more quickly if I would relinquish him temporarily. Carol too assured me that he would be well cared for and that I could take advantage of the opportunity to rest.

Begrudgingly, I handed him to the volunteer, reassuring him that I'd locate him inside the airport soon.

Finally, when each baby, toddler, and child had been taken from the plane, the escorts were allowed to get off to rest.

Chapter Fifteen

We could hardly believe the sight that greeted us. Hundreds of children and volunteers crowded every inch of the terminal. I pushed my way through with Carol trying to locate Mitchell. I knew my friend was too polite to complain about my compulsion to find him instead of resting as we had been advised to do. Clowns, balloons, and tables of food welcomed the children. While I admitted the gesture was lovely, I thought the bedlam added too much to an already confusing situation. My worries grew as I pressed harder into the throng. I couldn't find my son!

Then, there he was, smiling in the arms of a volunteer. It felt wonderful to hold him again as we stood on the balcony and looked down at wall-to-wall children and adults. The noise of crying, laughter, and talking was deafening.

Darn! I was feeling weak again, so I returned Mitchell to his caregiver and found the nearest bathroom.

We'd had no sleep since leaving the Philippines, and the hectic task of caring for so many babies on the plane left us exhausted.

"Before we rest I want to call Mark." I looked at my watch and figured he would be home.

"I made my share of phone calls before we left," Carol laughed. "I don't think I'll make any more for a while!"

The noise around the phone booth was so loud I had to shout instructions to the operator.

"Mark doesn't even know I've got our son," I said to Carol nervously. "He has no idea I'm bringing him home."

I had rehearsed in my mind how I would tell him the wonderful news, but when I heard his voice answer the phone I could only blurt out, "Honey, this is LeAnn," and I started to cry.

I could hear him repeating my name as he too sobbed. I tried to compose myself so I could tell him about Mitchell, but the tears were uncontrollable.

Then, still crying, he said, "Just tell me you're bringing me our son."

"Yes. Yes. Yes," I cried as my heart nearly burst with excitement and love.

Our tears blended with laughter as we talked with anticipation of being together soon.

Unbridled joy filled me as Carol and I lay on the floor of the airport balcony with our flight bags as pillows and attempted to sleep.

Two hours later, all escorts were advised to board the plane and prepare for the boarding of the children. One by one the children were gathered and returned through the back door of the plane, then placed into their original seats by the volunteers who then left through the front plane door. I nervously waited for Mitchell. Finally I saw him being carried toward me. He beamed his precious smile.

"This is some baby you have here," the volunteer said. "You're sure lucky."

"You have no idea," I said as I snatched him back into my arms.

Chapter Sixteen

We were headed for Travis Air Force Base in San Francisco. It was to be the holding area for all the children from different agencies coming to the United States from Vietnam.

Carol chatted with an American man sitting in front of her. He seemed at ease handling the four babies next to him. One of the infants appeared newborn, frail, and tiny. She was very dark skinned with lots of straight, black hair. When we first left Clark, the man had seemed insecure about caring for such a small baby, but by then he was handling her with confidence. He was a short, stout, bald man in his early sixties. He told Carol he had worked for over twenty years in Saigon, and it had become his home. His eyes were red as he told her about the young, beautiful, Vietnamese woman with whom he had fallen in love and of the pain he felt in having to leave her behind. He said, "Since so many Vietnamese men are dead, she could love even an old codger like me." Now only retirement awaited him back home.

He also had a seven-year-old girl in his care. Her short, black, hair was in a pixie cut framing her face and her serious, dark eyes. She produced a tablet and paper from her bag and began writing in her native language, filling the page.

"She is really brilliant!" the old man exclaimed with the pride of a father. "I've only known her these few hours but you can tell how very smart she is." The child wrote on the page continuously. What was she writing? What did she have to say? It was impossible to imagine the stories captured in her mind and on her paper.

The spirit aboard the plane grew increasingly lighthearted as we grew nearer our destination. The escorts oohed and aahed over Mitchell, Personality, and the other children. Three doctors on board made rounds regularly during the flight. One gave the little boy Carol was caring for some phenobarbital since he continually cried and contorted. They believed he was retarded and was certainly confused about what was happening to him. He finally fell asleep in her lap.

During one of many diaper changes, I found dark bruise-like spots on Mitchell's hips and lower back.

"Those were bruises all right," said one escort. Another volunteer added an explanation. "It seems the Vietnamese believe in unhealthy spirits and beat on the backs of little ones to rid them from their bodies."

My heart ached at the thought of Mitchell having endured such treatment. As I sadly repeated this story to those around me, a physician overheard the explanation.

"Those are Mongolian spots," he offered with a grin. "Simply a pigmentation noted on the skin of many of Asian descent. It's normal. He'll grow out of it."

"Is there no end to my naïveté?" I wondered out loud.

"Let's check him out," he offered with a grin. Placing his stethoscope on Mitchell's chest and abdomen, he listened for what seemed to be a long time. Returning the stethoscope to his pocket, he smiled. "He's a healthy one," he said with the familiar reassurance of a pediatrician. He commented that Mitchell's features were not strongly Vietnamese and guessed that he was at least one quarter French or Amerasian.

Amerasian.

What if only one flight had been allowed out as was threatened, and what if I hadn't gone back for him? Would he have survived if left behind?

Chapter Sixteen

I quickly forced those thoughts from my mind.

There was a chorus of sighs of relief as the plane's wheels
screeched on the California runway. Back on the U.S. main-
land. Almost home!

Again, the Air Force took over and the babies were taken
from the plane one by one. If Mitchell was to be processed to
leave for Iowa, he too had to be taken with the other children. This time I did not resist.

The children were loaded on one bus and the adults followed on another to be transported to the Presidio in San
Francisco.

The ride was lovely and took us over the Golden Gate
Bridge. I felt like I was back in my tourist mode as the driver
pointed out Alcatraz.

The Presidio looked like a typical military station with its
stark, drab, gray exterior. The building that housed the babies
seemed large enough to hold the DC-10 we'd arrived on.
Instead of the neat rows of mattresses we'd found at Clark,
randomly placed mats covered the entire surface area of the
floor. There was no place to walk through the sea of talking
children and crying babies. The adults were screaming also to
be heard above the noise. Toys, clothes, and supplies were
readily available, but much less organized than at Clark.

Bedlam reigned.

Literally hundreds of children filled the building as they
were brought in for processing from every agency. Headquarters for each agency were established at tables adjacent to
their children. It took us awhile tiptoeing through the congestion before we found FCVN's area.

There, yelling and waving their arms at us, were Cheryl
Markson and Carol Westlake.

"Welcome to Operation Babylift!" Carol shouted above
the chaos.

They had heard about Mitch and embraced me with exu-
berance. So much had happened since they had handed me

147

that forty-pound duffel bag and $10,000 in Denver.

Was that just one week ago?

They were busy with the job of organizing dossiers and making arrangements for escorts to take the children to pre-assigned homes across the country. A new, and as-yet unoccupied, nursing home in Denver had volunteered to house the children of FCVN until homes were assigned.

The first order of business, of course, was to find Mitchell. This chaos was unlike any we had experienced so far. Cheryl and Carol sent us in the general direction.

"Look for green ID bracelets!" she called out with a laugh. We found him being examined by one of the many volunteer physicians. He smiled at his mom.

"He's a healthy one," the doctor assured me. I had questions I wanted to ask him but he excused himself to tend to some infants who were sick after the long flight.

I carried Mitchell and introduced him to Carol and Cheryl. In spite of the obvious work begging for their attention, they stopped instantly to meet my son. Having previously adopted children through FCVN, they both readily identified with my feelings.

"I can't wait to see our new daughter Mai," Cheryl's tired face lit up. "I talked with Cherie back in Saigon. Mai will be on a plane within a few days."

Carol and I listened as Cheryl and "the other Carol" told us that four of Cherie's kids and the Johnson trio would be arriving later that day. Would we escort them to their grandparents near our homes in Iowa?

After all she had done for me, I would do anything to help Cherie Clark.

"She has another planeload of orphans leaving today and plans to stay there and keep working till they're all out!" Cheryl said, shaking her head in admiration and wonderment. "If anyone can do it, she can."

Then Cheryl lowered her voice. "There was a bomb threat here just before you came," she said.

Chapter Sixteen

"A bomb threat!" Carol exclaimed putting her hand over her mouth. "We've got to get out of here!"

"It was quietly investigated and no bomb was found," Cheryl told her. "Another caller said, 'Dump the little _____ in the ocean!' "

After working so hard to bring the children to the United States it was impossible for me to understand how anyone could feel that way. "Someone called them the unloved reminders of an unloved war," Cheryl added.

Our eagerness to go back to Iowa was evident. We talked with Cheryl about the fastest way to do so. Our part of the mission seemed to be completed. There wasn't even anything we could do to assist with the chaos at Presidio. So Carol and I headed for our motel to get some rest. I was frustrated to learn I still couldn't take Mitchell. Government regulations required him to stay at the Presidio with the other airlift babies. As we climbed the worn concrete steps to our second-story room, I realized how severely the dysentery had lessened my endurance.

Once inside, I collapsed onto a blessedly clean bed while Carol called Al and told him about the flight times for our planned arrival in Cedar Rapids the next day. Al gladly agreed to call Mark. Next, Carol telephoned her sister. Carol had told me how she desperately wanted to ease the pain that had scarred their relationship before she had left for Saigon. I heard Carol's side of the conversation as she reached Suzanne and arranged to meet her for dinner. Though I was invited to join them, I knew I was not strong enough physically or emotionally to deal with Suzanne again. Instead, I wished Carol well, then quickly fell asleep.

The sound of Carol's key in the door woke me.

"How'd it go?" I sat up groggily and turned on the lamp beside me.

"I don't know," Carol answered as she sat on the edge of her bed. "She said she was glad I'm home safely. But even when I told her about everything that happened this week, I continued to get the message that she perceived the trip as foolish and risky." She kicked her shoes off and smiled. "But, you know, I didn't feel threatened this time."

I saw then that more than one mission had been well accomplished.

The car horn honked.

We descended the steps of the motel to receive final instructions about the care, keeping, and delivery of eight children.

Ross placed Mitchell in my arms.

This time to stay.

Ultimately, the plan was to meet Steve Johnson's parents at the Cedar Rapids Airport. They would be caring for their twin grandsons, Anthony and Christopher, and ten-year-old Jackie. They agreed to take Cherie's four children, Beth, Dan, Ron, and Brian, to their grandparents who lived nearby.

The last pieces of luggage were placed in the back of the station wagon. Ross slammed it closed and turned to us.

How could I say good-bye to someone who had impacted my life so powerfully?

"Thanks for everything, Ross," I began, my voice cracking. "Never could have done it without ya," I added with a little laugh. I hugged him a long time, fearing that when I let him go, I would never see him again. "Keep in touch. You're an important part of our lives now." I forced a deep breath.

His eyes were filled with tears. "I'm so happy for you," he said his attention turning to Mitchell. "He's quite a boy. Good-bye little friend." He shook Mitchell's small hand.

"Tell Sister Therese good-bye for us," Carol said. We were disappointed that her work at the Presidio didn't allow us a final farewell.

I gave Ross a parting hug and kiss on the cheek and silently slid into the back seat, my emotions in turmoil once more.

Cheryl drove us to the San Francisco airport. There she introduced us to a politician from Nebraska and the two

Vietnamese children he and his wife were to adopt. He had gone to Saigon to personally escort the six-year-old brother and sister home. Their big, dark eyes still reflected bewilderment at the sudden and enormous changes in their lives.

Cheryl was allowed to board the plane with us to help get the eight children settled in their seats. An off-duty flight attendant from United had volunteered to help as an escort. He seemed at ease holding Anthony, one of the one-year-old Johnson twins. We hugged Cheryl good-bye and settled in for the first leg of the trip.

The two-hour flight was uneventful. The babies were fed and slept while the older children enjoyed drinking pop and eating peanuts. Well behaved, they amused themselves with small toys and books they had with them, seemingly taking this adventure in stride.

When we arrived at Stapleton International Airport in Denver, Carol and I gathered the children and moved together through the terminal. I felt like a shepherd herding her flock as I coaxed and signaled the children to follow. United Airlines was providing free fare for Vietnamese orphans from various agencies as well as their escorts. Many were arriving in the Denver hub simultaneously. There were babies, children, and escorts everywhere.

As we moved to the next gate to board our plane to Cedar Rapids, Carol looked around. "Where's Anthony?"

Neither the flight attendant escort—nor Anthony—were anywhere in sight.

"Oh, no, we can't have lost Anthony!" I moaned.

"This cannot be!" Carol pleaded.

"They must have gone with another group!"

Frantically, Carol explained the situation to the man at the United Airlines information desk. He understood our concern and quickly called someone in authority. Immediately he paged the escort using only his first name and a description of the baby.

"Why didn't we get his last name?" Carol lamented.

"How could we let this happen?" I repeated as I recalled the promise of safekeeping I had pledged to the twins' parents.

We tried to console each other and remain calm although we knew the minutes were ticking away toward departure.

The airline official advised us to go to the boarding gate. He assured us he would do everything possible to locate Anthony and have him brought to us. He added that he would even hold the plane for a while. We found the gate and tried to focus our attentions toward offering the other children the reassurance we so badly needed ourselves.

The final call for our flight was announced. Carol helped me settle the seven children in their seats, then she went back into the terminal to wait for Anthony.

Within a few minutes, another official came to tell me that Anthony and his escort had been located. I breathed a great sigh of relief. They had mistakenly joined a group of escorts and orphans going to Fitzsimmons Army Hospital. United was sending someone to intercept that bus and return them to the airport. The man said he would hold the flight as long as possible. If they did not return soon, United would put Anthony and Carol up in a motel until the next flight to Cedar Rapids left in the morning.

Carol came back on the plane to convince me that she was all right with the possibility of yet another delay, and was prepared to spend the night in Denver with Anthony, if necessary. We hugged briefly, blinking back tears.

"We'll be fine," we exchanged our oft-repeated words.

I sat nervously on board as the pilot explained the delay to the other passengers. After another fifteen minutes, he announced that we could wait no longer.

"Please, please, don't take off yet," I begged the attendant. "Wait just a few more minutes." I explained how Carol and I had been together on a nine days journey and how unfair it would be to leave without her. She compassionately explained that it was impossible to wait any longer, that the rest of the passengers had schedules as well.

She gave me a sympathetic smile, then returned to the front of the cabin where she began instructing the passengers on the use of the oxygen masks, escape exit locations, and how to use the seat as a flotation device.

I wanted to yell, "Stop!" I had heard that spiel too many times in the previous four days. "Like I need a flotation device over Nebraska," I grumbled.

As the plane taxied down the runway for takeoff, I choked back tears. I held Mitchell on my lap and glanced back to where Cherie's four kids sat calmly in the seats directly behind me. They were being flown halfway around the world away from their parents, but nothing seemed to faze them. They had no doubt learned to be trusting and flexible. Across the aisle from me sat the politician and his two adopted children. He seemed impatient with them.

Carol watched the plane taxi down the runway. "I can't believe the way this is turning out," she whispered to herself as she followed the official to his office to wait for Anthony and get her tickets and stipend for the night at the motel.

The United official sat at his desk and made the necessary arrangements. Sitting on the straight metal chair in the stark office, she tried to take a few deep breaths to help her deal calmly with the situation. She knew Al would already be on his way to Cedar Rapids, anticipating their reunion. She had been so very close to home. It seemed the cruelest time for yet another delay.

After about fifteen minutes of small talk with the official the escort arrived with Anthony. The toddler flashed a big smile of contentment, as only a chubby-faced one-year-old could. His big, trusting, brown eyes were wide open as he held out his arms for Carol to take him. She couldn't help smiling in return.

"I guess it's you and me tonight."

The flight attendant apologized, obviously genuinely chagrined. Carol assured him that she understood.

A few minutes later, she sat alone waiting for the van to pick them up. Her arms were sore from holding the toddler and the heavy bag stuffed with his diapers and formula.

Together they checked into the hotel and made it safely to their room. While Anthony happily played on the carpeted floor by the bed, Carol phoned the Cedar Rapids airport and had Al paged.

"I have some bad news," she began. "I'm still in Denver." He sounded annoyed but his response softened to disappointment as Carol explained what had happened. He then told her that airport officials there in Iowa had told him there was a bomb threat at the airport because we were bringing Vietnamese children. The airport had been thoroughly checked but there had been no evacuation.

There it was again. Another threat to kill Vietnamese babies . . . and those who brought them.

"I'm sorry I won't see you and the boys tonight," she said. "I love you all. I can't wait to get home." Carol put the phone back on the cradle. She felt ready to be done with this adventure.

While she knew it wasn't Al's intention, being told about the bomb threat frightened her. She had planned to take Anthony to dinner in the hotel dining room but decided not to for his protection.

"Am I paranoid, or what?" she said out loud. "You may never get room service hot dogs again." He smiled. "It's hard to feel distressed with you around."

He reached for her face and she laughed. "We'll just try to relax and make the best of it."

After dinner, Carol prepared for bed since their flight was to leave very early the next morning, but Anthony wanted nothing to do with the crib that had been sent up. He stood by the rail and bawled. Carol laid him in bed next to her and talked to him quietly as she patted his back. They were both asleep within minutes.

Chapter Seventeen

Less than an hour after our takeoff from Denver, our plane landed in Lincoln, Nebraska. The politician and his children got off and several other people boarded. I recognized one as a newscaster from WMT-TV in Cedar Rapids. I was surprised when, after takeoff, he came to my seat, squatted in the aisle, and introduced himself. He asked if he could ask me a few questions. I declined his offer. He explained that this story had become important in Iowa. Many people were very supportive of our efforts during the airlift and would be eager to hear an interview.

Choking with emotion, I explained that Carol had been left behind and I was too upset to do an interview. He continued to persuade me and finally I agreed out of a sense of obligation.

I had never been interviewed before and found it peculiar that anyone would actually be interested in my activities. It felt awkward speaking into the microphone of the tape recorder. After I'd answered his questions for ten minutes or so, he thanked me warmly and took his seat again.

What a coincidence, I thought, that he and I happened to be on the same flight.

I rested my head back on the seat. The sadness of leaving Carol lessened as my anticipation of seeing Mark grew.

Would the girls be with him? It was past 9 o'clock. Probably not. I pictured him standing alone in the terminal, his arms outspread. I smiled as I envisioned us finally going home together.

"I've never seen so many lights or so much activity here," the pilot announced as we circled the airport. "There must be a celebrity on this flight."

I turned around, trying to look nonchalant as I gazed at the passengers and wondered who that might be.

I didn't recognize anyone famous.

When the plane landed and came to a stop, I wanted nothing more than to gather the children and run down the aisle and into the airport. Instead, I explained to them that we would let the other passengers deplane ahead of us so we could all stay together.

I didn't intend to lose any more kids.

As I made small talk with them, I realized that the younger ones didn't remember their grandparents. They all seemed a little perplexed, but had obviously learned during their time in Saigon that their mom knew best. Likewise, they obediently followed my instructions.

Finally the last of the passengers left the plane. I felt my heart accelerate as I took Mitchell into my arms. The attendant reminded me that it was cool in Cedar Rapids and gave me a blue flight blanket to put around him over his "summer" outfit. She had been helping with Anthony's twin, Christopher, during the flight, and offered to carry him off.

With the other children in tow, we descended the stairs of the plane. When my feet touched the runway, I was tempted again to sprint into the building and Mark's arms. It took all the restraint I could muster to walk slowly while speaking confidently to the kids about their visit with their grandparents.

I entered the building but couldn't see. Bright lights shone into my eyes. Confused, it took me a moment to grasp what was happening.

Chapter Seventeen

The large crowd and all the attention was for Carol and me! The children and I inched forward through the blinding glare. Then suddenly, Mark stepped through the camera lights with open arms, his smile shining across his face.

Mitchell and I stepped into this circle of quiet and held tight.

More than once in Saigon I had feared I would never again feel this embrace. Now I didn't want to let go.

The joy was overwhelming.

This was all I needed in the world.

My life was complete.

I stepped back so Mark could get a good look at his new son. In response, Mitch opened his arms and reached for his daddy. Mark's eyes brimmed with tears as he hugged him near.

A few feet past him, I saw my mom and my sisters, Mary and Theresa. They were there to support me, just as they had been all my life. They told me that Diane, having anticipated this media-laden reception, had stayed home with our daughters. I felt confused, like I was in a waking dream, as I embraced them and other relatives who had come to meet the plane.

Al came over and I tried to keep my composure as I started to explain why Carol was not with me. He hushed me and told me they had spoken on the phone. Concealing his obvious disappointment, he hugged me warmly.

Already the older Johnsons were holding Christopher and talking with the Clark kids. I made my way over to them and introduced myself. They were understanding about the mix-up with Anthony in Denver. I wanted to explain and to tell them about meeting their son Steve and about his wonderful volunteer work in Vietnam. But it was so hectic! Reporters with lights and microphones kept pushing their way into our conversation.

Mark was only a few steps away and I went to him.

He directed me down a corridor away from the crowds and

press. "You're going to have to trust me on this one, Honey," he said. "You're going to hold a press conference."

I couldn't believe my ears.

"Mark, I can't. I don't want to. I only want to go home."

"You have no idea what's been going on here since you've been gone. The newspapers and TV reporters have been calling Al and me day and night. This is the biggest story that's happened here in a long time. They've all promised that if you have a press conference and talk to them now, they'll leave us alone afterward."

By that time we had come to a large room filled with reporters. I saw a long table in the front with what appeared to be dozens of microphones all in a row.

Everything was happening so fast.

I wanted desperately to turn and leave, but knew I trusted Mark absolutely. He gave me a proud smile as he led me to my chair.

I stifled a laugh as I sat down in front of all those mikes and all those people. It seemed like something you would see on "Meet the Press," not something I should be doing. My laughter was stifled by sadness as I realized how much Carol belonged there too. I felt lonely without her and a bit guilty to be in such a limelight when she was not there to share it.

"How did you get involved in this airlift, Mrs. Thieman?"

"Where did all these babies come from?"

"Were you ever afraid?"

"Did you know about the planeload of babies that crashed? Were you there?"

"What was it like in Saigon?"

"Did any babies die?"

"Will you go back?"

I was surprised at my ability to answer each question articulately and calmly.

"The Vietnamese government accused the U.S. of kidnapping their orphans. Why do you think they're so reluctant to let them leave?"

"They prefer to take care of their own," I offered, recalling Cherie's explanation to me.

"Some say the United States is just trying to atone for its sins. What do you say to that?"

I responded quickly. "I don't think this is about appeasing American guilt. It's the basic decency of the American people. When they see a suffering child, they want to help. Remember too, these sentiments didn't just spring up overnight. For the adoptive parents, this process of bringing orphans to the United States has been underway for months, even years."

"What will happen to all these babies? Did you know the State Department set up a toll-free number for would-be adoptive families? They were getting 1,000 calls a minute!"

"In Vietnam we had no idea this was getting so much attention in the States. I was told there was a plan for 2,000 orphans to come out, but most have already been assigned homes."

Then a question came about Carol's absence. My voice broke as I explained about the mix-up in Denver.

"I think her staying behind with Anthony is truly a tribute to the kind of giving and loving person she is," I answered. "She deserves to be sitting here as much as I do." I gazed at Al's kind smile.

Mark and I took turns holding Mitchell as the questions kept firing. Mitchell smiled and patted his hands and seemed intrigued with the lights.

Finally, Mark said that was enough and ended the session. Still, persistent reporters called out questions and attempted to follow us to the parking lot.

Mark turned and reminded them firmly of the deal that had been promised, and they retreated as we made our way to the car.

"I can't wait to go home with you," I said softly as I hugged Mark again before getting into the car.

"We're not going home," he apologized. He knew I'd be

disappointed. "We're going to your mom's." He explained the badgering he had experienced from the reporters the past few days. He didn't trust that they would honor the agreement to respect our privacy in Iowa City.

I was indeed disappointed.

This was not at all how I had envisioned our homecoming. Yet going to Mom's where I'd be pampered and nurtured and surrounded by my big, loving family did sound appealing.

During the thirty-minute ride to Vinton alone with Mark and Mitchell I felt carefree. There was so much we both wanted to say, but neither of us knew where to begin. Mostly, I just wanted to hear all about him and the girls. No one had told Angela and Christie about my bringing Mitchell home. He thought it would be a wonderful thing to share with them in person as they did love "surprises." I knew they would be asleep at Diane's since it was nearly midnight, but I wanted to go just to see them, not wake them.

Until I entered Mom's house.

Something inside me clicked off. The stress that had provided the energy to keep going was suddenly gone. Exhaustion immobilized me. It didn't take much to convince me that I should wait until morning to see our girls.

We made Mitchell a mattress of blankets on the floor next to our bed in the guest room. Mom apologized for the poor accommodations for him on short notice. I laughed as I tried to explain how he was used to sleeping on mats on the floor throughout this trip and began to tell them about the Center in Saigon with scores of babies all over the floor.

A part of me wanted to stay up all night and talk endlessly about all that had happened. I knew they would have listened if my fatigue had not made it impossible.

After hugging Mom and thanking her, I shut off the light and slipped into bed with Mark. I felt the strong, safe embrace I had longed for so often in the past ten days. It was then that the tears I had suppressed throughout this incredible day were poured out.

Chapter Seventeen

* * *

The wake-up call came early and Carol prepared for the flight home. Anthony crawled around happily as Carol dressed and applied her makeup. She carried him through the motel shielding his face with a blanket. The van delivered them back to Stapleton Airport and soon they were boarding the plane for their flight to Cedar Rapids.

Carol relaxed into the seat by the window and rocked Anthony in her arms. He was soon asleep. As she looked down at Anthony she thought about the hundreds of babies and the little dark-haired girl. It was difficult for her to believe that there actually had been a bomb threat at the Cedar Rapids Airport. She pulled the blanket closer around Anthony's face.

"Are there really people out there who would want to hurt Vietnamese babies or me and my children?" she whispered to the sleeping child in her arms. "Is LeAnn jeopardizing her family by bringing Mitchell into their home?" She closed her eyes and drifted to sleep.

The plane landed at the Cedar Rapids airport. Gingerly, she walked through the door of the terminal and into bright lights. Al had told her about the press the night before, so she was prepared for the onslaught of reporters. She looked eagerly for her family and smiled when she saw Al, Chris, and Chad.

"Hi Mommy!" the two-year-old beamed.

In an emotional reunion of hugs and kisses, she repeated, "I sure did miss you. I love you all so much."

Anthony's grandparents greeted him happily. His big, dark eyes seemed to ask what was going on, yet he quietly accepted their affection and welcoming arms. They visited briefly as Carol explained the confusion in Denver.

Two reporters from Cedar Rapids TV stations asked Carol if they could have a short interview. She said good-bye to the Johnsons and gave Anthony a quick, final hug.

161

Sitting in the waiting area of the airport with Al and the boys, she described the experience as a "wonderful nightmare."

"It was a nightmare in some ways, but it was also wonderful to be part of bringing the children to the U.S. Seeing what so many were going through and knowing there are families wanting them makes it very worthwhile."

They asked about the military's role in the airlift. "The Air Force was great. Very organized. Boy, we were happy to see them when we were leaving Saigon!" Then she added, "I think I've experienced every possible emotion. There is definitely a sense that the country will fall soon."

The reporters thanked her for her time and welcomed her back. Al had gotten the suitcases and the boxes the night before so they went right to the car. Al carried wide-eyed Chad and Chris took his mom's hand and scurried along. As they walked arm in arm she declared, "I'm so happy to be home safe and sound."

While they drove home she repeated several times how glad she was to see them. She wondered out loud how our family was doing with Mitchell. She was thankful she had not given in to her fears and admitted a sense of accomplishment, yet a sense of loss that it was over. Al told her about all the cards and calls from family and friends. They joked that she and I were Iowa City celebrities. The boys talked on about the decorations and banners they had colored for her welcome-home party.

"Hi Mommy! Hi Mommy!" Chad repeated periodically.

"How'd you like war?" Chris asked with excitement.

As they chattered, she rested her head back on the seat. How wonderful it was to hear their voices again.

"You know, Al, I think it's appropriate that LeAnn and I arrived home separately," she said softly. "We were linked so closely in the journey and the adventure, yet we each have our own personal story to tell . . . our own separate victory."

162

Chapter Seventeen

I was up several times in the night with stomachaches and diarrhea, but still managed to sleep until the late hour of 9. I woke in Mark's arms and grinned down at our son sleeping peacefully beside our bed. I was entranced in the moment as I lay there watching his little chest rise and fall with each breath.

Then I heard my girls' voices. I fumbled putting my robe on and rushed to the living room while Mitchell and Mark continued to sleep soundly.

"Mommy! Mommy!" Angela and Christie chimed. I stooped to hug them both at the same time and they bounced into my arms. How wonderful to feel their chubby little arms around me. I couldn't let go. I quietly thanked God for this moment, one that I had once doubted possible. As they hugged me longer and harder, I pretended to fall back onto the floor while they smothered me with kisses.

Finally I stood to embrace my sister. "How can I thank you?" I choked in a whisper.

"No, how can I thank you?" she said, squeezing me even harder. "Having them with me when you were so far away was my salvation." The glow of relief on her face told me there had been worry she would not express.

"Aunt Diane said we could come see you as soon as we woke up. We didn't even eat our breakfast!" Angela giggled.

So we walked to Grandma's kitchen in our usual fashion, with Angela holding tightly to my left hand and Christie clinging to my right leg. As they munched their cereal I delighted in listening to the tales of their great "vacation."

"Aunt Diane reads stories at bedtime every night just like you, Mommy," Angela reported. I glanced at Diane hoping my eyes reflected my gratitude and love.

"We made faces with our macaroni!" Christie exclaimed, milk dripping down her chin.

"And we colored you a welcome home sign," Angela added.

Then, there he was.

Mitchell had crawled from the bedroom to the kitchen doorway.

Before I could speak any words of explanation, Angela beamed at me and said, "This must be my brother!"

Indeed.

Epilogue

The excitement and joy we felt being a part of the Vietnam Orphan Airlift was relived as we wrote this book and especially the epilogue. Contacting these remarkable people again after two decades was like writing another final chapter.

LeAnn and Carol

ROSS MEADOR returned to Vietnam immediately and remained there after FCVN's third and final flight out. He tried to distribute remaining supplies and arrange for the evacuation of some of the staff. He recalls that on April 28th the ground rumbled with the bombing of Ton Son Nhut Airport and he sheltered himself on the kitchen floor at the Center. He was awakened the next morning by gunshots. This time it was no joke . . . no young soldiers playing games. He looked over the balcony to see ten young men in black pajamas break open the gate and run into the courtyard toward the building. He shot a pistol into the air and scared them away, then fled in the van, past convoys of tanks and constant gunfire, to the U.S. Embassy. Late that night, from the embassy roof, he boarded the final U.S.

helicopter to leave Vietnam. While guns fired relentlessly below, the chopper zigzagged its way to the U.S.S. *Midway*. Ross looked down to see much of the city on fire.

On April 30th, 1975, South Vietnam fell to the communists.

After nearly a year of traveling through Thailand, Asia, and Africa, Ross returned to California and started college. His studies were interrupted several times when he joined FCVN in Korea then Cherie Clark in India doing orphan relief work. In 1986 he completed his law degree and is currently working for a firm in Seoul, South Korea.

SISTER THERESE LE BLANC returned to Vietnam with Ross and Cherie to rescue the final planeload of orphaned infants and older children. She recalls the events of that evacuation to be far more chaotic and dangerous than ours. At one time Air Force personnel stood guard with automatic weapons to assure their safety during the departure. She rejoined the staff in Denver to assist with the placement of the children. Later she joined Cherie Clark in India for five weeks to establish a foundation for orphan relief there. She returned to the States to attend nursing school but postponed her studies to be a chaplain in a psychiatric unit for four years. For the past fourteen years she has been the chaplain at a physical rehabilitation facility.

She fondly recalls her work with the Babylift as the "best of my life!"

CHERYL MARKSON has dedicated the past twenty-three years to FCVN, now Friends of Children of Various Nations. She's modest about her role as agency director for the past twenty years, but admits she has facilitated nearly 5,000 adoptions during that time. She reminds us that adoption is only one form of aid and FCVN works with programs for orphan relief in India, Thailand, Costa Rica, Mexico, Korea, Slovakia, Russia, China, and now again in Vietnam.

After Mai's arrival, her family adopted five more Amerasian children from Korea bringing the count at family mealtime to thirteen!

CHERIE CLARK, and 150 orphans, were on the last U.S. plane to leave South Vietnam under a cloud of smoke and panic. She worked several months with FCVN in Denver, then traveled to Guam to help with the Vietnamese refugees. She went on to visit Thailand, Colombia, then India where she settled for fifteen years. There she established the International Mission of Hope in Calcutta working for orphan relief and adoption. In 1988 she returned to Vietnam with Cheryl and Mick Markson to visit the destitute orphanages and nuns they had once worked with so closely. Because much of the city was ruined and many of the streets had been renamed, they had difficulty finding the former FCVN Center. When at last they did, they found it to be even more beautiful than before! They toured the familiar rooms that now serve as a primary school for children in that area.

Cherie describes that trip as a "reunion of sorrows . . . a promise reborn." She established the International Mission of Hope in Ho Chi Minh City where she continues to help the suffering children.

STEVE JOHNSON left Vietnam with his wife Carol the week before the country fell. They were reunited with their three sons in northern Illinois where Steve,

CHRISTOPHER, and ANTHONY live today. Chris played football, baseball, and soccer all through school yet found time to develop his musical talents. His leading roles in musicals and concert choirs led him to Northern Illinois University. Tony was an avid soccer player and played summer league baseball. He completed his sophomore year at Northern Illinois University.

Steve enjoys his work as the Director of External Programs for the College of Liberal Arts and Sciences at Northern Illinois University. He has returned to Vietnam on two occasions and rediscovered the orphanage where he first found his sons.

CAROL KIM resides in California where she continues to perform as a singer.

Epilogue

THUY (Le-Thi Bach-Thuy) left her home country with FCVN's final flight of orphans. She was then reunited with her two children who had escaped Vietnam on one of the earlier flights. Her continued work for FCVN was vital as she translated documents and counseled frightened children in their native language. Thuy spent countless months establishing a Vietnam Cultural Resource Center for the children and their adoptive families. Newsletters included stories about their homeland, holiday customs, Vietnamese songs, and family adjustment suggestions.

She went to Colorado Women's College to complete her bachelor's degree in sociology and graduated in 1980 with a Master of Social Work from the University of Denver. Immediately following her graduation she married a Vietnamese psychologist, Dr. Tran Nhu Choung, and resettled in Tampa, Florida. Together they opened their own business in the immigration field, assisting aliens in preparing documents to become permanent citizens. They were enthusiastically involved in the Vietnamese community, providing counseling and helping refugee resettlements throughout Florida.

Their daughter is a second-year medical student at the University of Florida. Their son resides in Gainesville where he is married and has a son. Thuy was widowed in 1994 and continues the work she and her husband began ten years ago.

DR. CUONG fled Vietnam and has a medical practice in the Midwest.

KIEU, the nurse, escaped Vietnam with the last planeload of orphans and settled in the Northwest.

169

PHOUNG, the secretary, was on the last flight out of Vietnam and made her home on the East Coast.

MAI MARKSON, now Maily Wong, lives in the Bay Area in California with her husband, Ron, and their son, Rudy. Maily perceives her adoption by the Marksons as something to "treasure for a lifetime." She writes, "It's definitely been rewarding to be brought up in an ethnic family background. For all the adopted children out there, you're definitely special because you are loved by somebody special. Looking back after all these years gone by, I thank God for taking me where I am today, blessing myself and my family for all that we have today.

"Now and then I catch myself with tears in my eyes and feeling so happy to know that I am blessed with my wonderful American family.

"Vietnam will always remain in my heart for it is my proud country."

THE GIRL WITH THE SHAVED HEAD is JEN-
NIFER LIN BERGNER. The frailty of her infancy was
not apparent as spectators cheered her outstanding ath-
letic ability from grade school through high school. In
spite of her tiny frame and slender features, her agility
and speed amazed her opponents on basketball and vol-
leyball courts. Her excellent grades led her to the University of Colorado where she is considering a degree in
psychology or education. Her five brothers and one sister describe her as a happy, easygoing person with lots
of friends. Her parents describe her simply "a true gift
from God."

MAGGIE and JOANIE, the babies left behind, de-
parted with Sister Therese on the third and final FCVN
flight out of Vietnam. Sister Therese recalls the week
before they left, Maggie's skin and features resembled
that of an old woman. She lay like a rag doll in Sister's

arms, too weak to cry. "But she was a fighter!" Sister Therese boasts, and her condition improved in time to bring her out.

Joanie was fed with an eyedropper when IVs were not available. When she arrived in the Philippines, she was cared for by a U.S. sailor heading for the States. He doted over her like a daddy and tenderly cared for her until she arrived in California.

MITCHELL THIEMAN was admitted to the hospital with a serious viral infection a few weeks after he arrived. He recovered quickly and has been incredibly healthy since. Growing up he spent his boundless energy mercilessly teasing his adoring sisters and playing city league baseball. (He even scored the winning run in the Little League tournament!) In high school he excelled in many areas including student council and forensics. Mitch completed his freshman year at a Colorado university and works to finish his schooling.

Epilogue

His middle name is Thai . . . Vietnamese for peace. He continues to develop the traits he had when he picked his mom — his gifts of love, wit, independence, compassion, charm . . .

U.S. Government investigations determined the C-5A was not sabotaged or shot down. A mechanical problem caused the crash.

There were 2,700 orphans brought to the United States during "Operation Babylift."

Carol has given LeAnn orange jellybeans every April 1st since 1975!